THE EDUCATION REFORM ACT:
CHOICE AND CONTROL

THE EDUCATION REFORM ACT:
CHOICE AND CONTROL

Edited by

Denis Lawton

Professor of Education and Director
University of London Institute of Education

Hodder & Stoughton

LONDON SYDNEY AUCKLAND TORONTO

British Library Cataloguing in Publication Data
The Education Reform Act: choice and control
  1. England. Education. Law. Education Act 1988
  I. Lawton, Denis, *1931–*
  344.204'7
  ISBN 0 340 51154 0

First published 1989

Typeset by Taurus Graphics, Abingdon, Oxon.
Printed in Great Britain for Hodder and Stoughton Educational, a
division of Hodder and Stoughton Ltd, Mill Road, Dunton Green,
Sevenoaks, Kent by Athenaeum Press Ltd, Newcastle upon Tyne.

Contents

Notes on Contributors

TESSA BLACKSTONE, Master of Birbeck College, was a member of the Think Tank from 1975 to 1978. She has also been a Professor of Educational Administration (at the Institute of Education) and Director of Education for the Inner London Education Authority.

MAURICE KOGAN, Professor of Government and Social Administration at Brunel University, has written extensively on the politics of education, and is acknowledged as an intellectual authority on Higher Education.

DENIS LAWTON, Director of the Institute of Education University of London, was formerly Professor of Education and Head of the Curriculum Studies Department. His books include *Education, Culture and the National Curriculum*, Hodder and Stoughton (1989).

STUART MACLURE, Editor of *The Times Educational Supplement*, is well-known for his writings on the history of education. He has also written a guide to the Education Reform Act *Education Re-formed*, Hodder and Stoughton (1988).

DESMOND NUTTALL, Head of Research and Statistics at the Inner London Education Authority, was formerly Professor of Educational Psychology at the Open University. He has conducted extensive research into a variety of aspects of assessment. His books include *Assessing Educational Achievement*, Falmer Press (1986).

Foreword

The purpose of this book is not to attempt a comprehensive analysis of the whole 1988 Education Act, but to allow five educationists with very different backgrounds and interests to focus on aspects of the legislation within the general theme of 'choice and control'. (The task of reviewing and commenting on the whole Act has been undertaken by Stuart Maclure in a separate volume – *Education Re-formed.*)

The five discussion papers began as a lecture series at the Institute of Education, University of London during February and March 1988; the idea of responding to the Education Bill by means of a series of lectures was Professor Basil Bernstein's, who also planned and organised the events, and suggested the overarching title for the series 'choice and control'. Rather than publish the five Papers in exactly the form in which they were given – that is, as lectures about the Bill – it was decided to wait until the Bill had received Royal Assent, and then to invite the five authors to revise their Papers, taking into account any significant changes that had taken place during the transition from Bill to Act. All five lecturers readily agreed to undertake whatever rewriting might be necessary. Thus we now have reflections on the 1988 legislation rather than what was proposed in 1987. It is fair to say that where the Government was persuaded to make any changes, it was at the level of detail rather than major principles.

Stuart Maclure had a difficult task because in addition to revising his lecture, he had also accepted an invitation from Hodder and Stoughton to write an account of the whole Act: inevitably there will be some overlap between the publications, although the purposes of the two books are very different.

Professor Denis Lawton
November 1988

Introduction

Denis Lawton

In 1979 the Conservative Party led by Mrs Margaret Thatcher won the General Election with a large majority. Since then, the 'Thatcher Government' has acquired a reputation for adhering to a variety of distinctive economic and social policies, many of which are associated with the diminution of state control. In education the picture is more complicated: the three Secretaries of State for Education since 1979, Mark Carlisle, Sir Keith Joseph and especially Kenneth Baker, have increased the amount of state control in education. To some extent this apparent contradiction may be explained as the power of the bureaucratic machine to continue with its own agenda, irrespective of what government happens to be in office; and it can be shown that since the mid-1970s the Department of Education and Science (DES) has consistently adopted policies of centralisation in areas such as teacher training, the school curriculum and educational expenditure. But the existence of DES centralism does not totally explain the contrast between the dominant Conservative social philosophy and its attitude to the education service since 1979. We have to look for additional explanations for the fact that the 1988 Act gives the Secretary of State hundreds of new powers.

One possible explanation is that the Conservative Government would prefer to loosen or even to abandon state control in education, but realises that this would be politically unpopular, and instead adopts the second best policy of 'value for money'; if there has to be a state system then it had better be tightly controlled. We have occasionally been reminded that less government does not necessarily mean weaker government.

Another plausible explanation is that ideological consensus is lacking on many social issues within the Conservative Party – including consensus on education. George and Wilding (1985) have contrasted the views of the 'anti-collectivists' and the 'reluctant collectivists' within the Party, for example. Thus the 1988 Act may be seen not as a coherent expression of Party policy, but as a messy compromise: some parts of the legislation appear to encourage 'freedom' and 'choice', other parts build up the bureaucratic machine to an extent that would have been unthinkable a few years ago.

One aspect of this lack of Conservative consensus relates to local education authorities (LEAs). A not insignificant group within the Conservative Party has a very strong interest in education at LEA level, sitting as members of education committees and taking considerable interest in local policy making. They are often resentful of any increase in central control exercised at the expense of local autonomy – some objected, for example, to making it possible for schools to opt out of LEA control and establish a direct link with the central authority. On the other hand, some Conservatives dislike the high spending metropolitan LEAs, and strongly support any devices such as rate-capping to trim local powers.

Our five contributors were asked to address their topics within the general theme 'choice and control'. In Chapter 1 Stuart Maclure begins by looking at several aspects of 'choice' in education. After 1988 some parents will be given more choice of schools, and schools will have the chance of opting out of LEA control. But does more choice for some mean less choice for others? And what is the cost to the planning of the system when, as Maclure puts it, LEAs are 'forced to plan by attrition instead of by more rational processes of decision making'. The 1988 Act certainly changes the existing scene very dramatically.

In Chapter 2, Denis Lawton strongly endorses the idea of a national curriculum, but finds the list of traditional subjects inadequate as a basis for planning a reformed curriculum. He looks at the ideological background to these ideas and highlights conflicts within the Conservative Party. He concludes that teachers will overcome the problems inherent in the national curriculum proposals, and will produce something better than many have predicted possible.

In Chapter 3, Desmond Nuttall focuses on the related question of national assessment. He looks critically but constructively at the work of the Task Group for Assessment and Testing (TGAT), and argues that teacher professionalism should be respected, not supplanted by the tests. He is also concerned about the publication of test results and of the market competition philosophy behind that aspect of the Act – perhaps of the whole Act.

In Chapter 4, Maurice Kogan analyses two models of Higher Education: the autonomous model of self-governance, and the managerialist model. The 1988 Act takes us in the direction of bureaucratic accountability. The question of tenure for academic staff may only be a symbolic issue, but other aspects of the Act such as contract funding may be of direct significance.

In Chapter 5, Tessa Blackstone points out that had the Government been intent on reforming the ILEA, other parts of the Act could have produced the desired results – for example, schools that felt oppressed by ILEA policies could opt out. But instead, abolition was regarded as necessary. In this case, control was preferred to leaving choice open. In many respects the ILEA represented qualities disliked by many Conservatives: it was a large, bureaucratic, planned and expensive system.

Finally, in Chapter 6, Lawton begins to analyse the importance of the idea of choice in education, and to examine whether the market is likely to be able to provide desirable choice more effectively than a planned educational system.

1

Parents and Schools: Opting In and Opting Out

Stuart Maclure

The Education Reform Act 1988 is the most important and far-reaching piece of educational law-making since the 1944 Education Act. Mr Kenneth Baker emphasised this in his opening speech in the Commons Second Reading debate when he said:

> 'Our education system has operated over the past 40 years on the basis of the framework laid down by Rab Butler's 1944 Act, which in turn built on the Balfour Act of 1902. We need to inject a new vitality into that system. It has become producer-dominated. It has not proved sensitive to the demands for change that have become ever more urgent over the past 10 years. This Bill will create a new framework, which will raise standards, extend choice and produce a better informed Britain.'

In going out of his modest way to invite comparison with Butler and Balfour, was Mr Baker over-playing his hand? Probably – this Act covers a much narrower front than the 1902 Act or the 1944 Act, but the implications are certainly far-reaching because it radically alters the power structure. It reshapes the role of the Secretary of State and the assumptions of the DES, cuts down the powers of the local education authorities, changes the functions of headteachers and governing bodies, and puts parents in a position to exercise more influence.

The Education Reform Act redesigns the educational chess

board. It does this in ways which bring new and uncertain consequences. It is not a blueprint for a settled future: it is a device – a dangerous or a brilliant device, according to your viewpoint – for stirring things up – putting all educational counters into play.

It requires no crystal ball to reach the conclusion that it will raise more questions than it settles. This is no bad thing, in the eyes of its authors – it is designed to shake the educational establishment out of its complacent slumbers. One way of doing this is by setting up a legislative framework which leaves the future up for grabs.

Opting In
(Education Reform Act, Chapter II, Sections 26–32 – The admission of pupils to county and voluntary schools)
The task of the legal draftsman was to ensure that, in future, all maintained schools accept a full complement of pupils, up to the limit of their physical capacity, unless they can satisfy the Secretary of State that they cannot accommodate this so-called standard number.

The actual legislation is complicated by the Secretary of State's desire to make it easy to increase the permitted maximum entry and hard to reduce it. To set an admissions figure below the standard number, a local authority (or in the case of a voluntary-aided school, a board of governors) will have to publish notices and go through the full public hoops, with objectors putting their case against such a reduction to the Secretary of State. It is then for him, in London, to decide the issue. Grammar schools will continue to be able to operate a policy of selection and limit their admissions to pupils who can satisfy their entry requirements.

Voluntary-aided schools are covered where they have an agreement with the local education authority designed to protect the schools' denominational ethos and to allow them to restrict access to pupils not belonging to their own religious group. If they do not already have such an agreement, one must be entered into.

The reasoning behind the proposal is beguilingly simple. The Government wants to put parents into a stronger position in relation to the education system. In part this springs from populist rhetoric: the analysis of the defects of the present education system which ministers have adopted, attributes many weaknesses to what Mr Baker calls the dominance of the producers. Giving more power to the consumers is a logical way to reduce that dominance. There is also the true perception that parents' encouragement and support are prime ingredients in successful education. Giving parents more power of choice could be a potent way of conscripting their commitment.

And beyond this, there is the ideological belief that education can acquire some of the benefits of a competitive market if consumers have more power to influence the producers by showing, actively, their preference for one school and one kind of education over another.

Giving parents an unrestricted right of access for their children to the school of their choice, until the last desk in that school is filled, is the way the Government has chosen to project these aims at the local level.

To gauge the impact of the change, we have to put these proposals in the perspective of earlier legislation. Under an Act of Parliament passed in 1980 (also brought forward by a Government headed by Mrs Thatcher) the arrangements for the allocation of pupils to schools set out in the 1944 Act, were revised. The context in which this took place was much affected by falling rolls – the working out in primary and secondary schools of the fall in the birth-rate between 1964 and 1977.

Demography always has a bearing on educational planning and administration – usually a bigger part than ideology. For thirty years, the education system was driven forward on the tide of expansion and the energy and the optimism which this evoked. Since the mid-1970s it has been the problems raised by a lengthy period of contraction which have dominated planning, the need to cope with a demographic trend which reflects a fall in the school population of nearly one-third – three million pupils – from peak to trough.

Falling rolls mean surplus school places unless or until schools are reorganised to take places out of service. At the time of the 1980 Act, two parallel policies were adopted. One was to cut back the provision. This went forward, unevenly throughout the country, and local education authorities have kept up with, or exceeded, the targets set by the Government for the elimination of empty classrooms through the closures and merger of schools and by the taking out of service of surplus buildings. By the time the Bill was published in 1987, more than 1.25 million places had been eliminated.

It was, however, recognised that it was not practicable to take out all surplus places as fast as pupil numbers declined. Nor, given the proverbial uncertainty of all demographic forecasting, would it be sensible to try to do so. There was, therefore, the expectation that, even if local authorities were prudent in reducing their stock of school buildings, it would still be necessary to manage a system in which there were more school places than pupils to fill them.

The second leg of the policy, therefore, was to give authorities more discretion over the number of pupils to be admitted to each school. This meant addressing the emotive question of how much choice parents should have in the matter of the placement of their children.

The 1944 Act had established parents' rights to express a preference about the schools their child should attend. Section 76 did this in the form of one of those grand declaratory but far from definitive expressions of good intention:

> 'In the exercise and performance of all powers and duties conferred and imposed on them by this Act, the Secretary of State and the local education authorities shall have regard to the general principle that so far as is compatible with the provision of efficient instruction and training and the avoidance of unreasonable public expediture, pupils are to be educated in accordance with the wishes of their parents.'

In practice, this was of limited use, though no doubt it helped to shape the policy of local authorities in the great majority of uncontentious cases. It did not prevent authorities most of the time treating each case on its educational and administrative merits. Parents' wishes were to be taken into account, but not treated as sovereign.

When confrontation did arise, however, certain defects in

administering the 1944 Act arose because the really persistent parent, who was prepared to keep his child out of school long enough to force the authority to prosecute, could usually get his own way in the end, even if the school of his choice was, technically, full up. Isolated cases of this nature were an irritation which exposed the inadequacy of the law and its enforcement.

The 1980 Act, therefore, set out to reform the procedure. The parents' right to choose (or, rather, express a preference which the local education authority had to take into account) was again guaranteed and local appeals committees were created to deal with disputed cases. And arrangements for the serving of school attendance orders were tightened up to remove the loophole by which stubborn parents could frustrate the purpose of the proceedings.

The most important sections of the 1980 Act, however, concerned the way of deciding how many pupils a school should be required to admit. Each school was given a 'standard number', based on the 1979–80 entry. But the local authority was accorded the power to fix an admission limit, up to 20 per cent below this number, at its own discretion. An even lower limit could be fixed, but only after publishing proposals and submitting these to the Secretary of State for his approval.

The 1980 Act, then, ostensibly put parental rights of choice up front, but in reality it was a way of curbing them more effectively. What the Education Reform Act now does is sweep away the discretionary element which has allowed local authorities to set aside parents' wishes. It expressly rejects any suggestion that efficiency or economy (however phrased) could constitute a valid reason for refusing a parent's demand for a child to attend a particular school. The only considerations which are to be considered are those which arise from the physical capacity of the school. This is spelled out: a Secretary of State who deviated from this in considering an application for a lower admissions number, would court an action for judicial review.

Since 1980, many local authorities have taken the opportunity presented by falling rolls to reduce the size of their larger secondary schools, and schools have got used to living in less crowded conditions. The space provision in many secondary schools built in the late 1960s to early 1970s became extremely tight and there are good reasons why many teachers welcomed the easement which the 1980 Act made possible.

Also, local education authorities have used their power to control intake to prevent highly popular schools from becoming uncomfortably full, while less popular schools become uneconomically and inefficiently small. Writing in *The Independent* soon after the Government's open enrolment proposals had been set out, Tim Brighouse, then Oxfordshire County Education Officer, gave as an example of the way the 1980 Act had been used, two secondary schools in the Oxfordshire town of Witney. One was a former grammar school, the other a former secondary modern school. As he put it:

> 'The ex-grammar school was sometimes (wrongly) perceived by the public to have a better reputation. In fact both schools were equally successful academically. Had the 1980 Act not existed, one of these perfectly good schools might have been crippled by innuendo and rumour . . . the other school would have become painfully overcrowded. As it was, each school prospered. The now expanding town needs two schools and has two good ones.'

Similar examples could be quoted from all over the country.

In considering what will be the likely consequences of the open enrolment sections of the 1988 Act, it has to be recognised that the local authority response has been almost uniformly hostile. On the other hand, I have heard one or two chief education officers say privately that in their areas it will be an inconvenience only affecting a few schools.

The local impact will undoubtedly vary. It will be most significant where reorganisation has been delayed and the standard numbers in many schools will be well above the current level of admission. But just how much effect these clauses will have on parental choice can only be estimated school by school, depending on the neighbourhood, the local transport arrangements competitive reputations, the standard of the buildings and so on.

Where there are many more places than pupils, schools will

be forced into even greater efforts to market themselves. Already, falling rolls have placed schools in a position where they are afraid that if they fail to attract their share of applicants they may cease to be viable. Open enrolment will reinforce this and force headteachers and their staff to pay a great deal of attention to public relations and the projection of the school's image in as favourable terms as possible.

The effect of the new regime of testing and assessment under the national curriculum will, of course, be given added importance when schools know that their published results will have to form part of their promotion (or relegation) campaign.

Now, all this will create a whole new competitive world for schools – a world in which there will certainly be losers as well as winners. Many members of the teaching profession will find the prospect eminently unattractive and fear, with what they believe they could show to be good reason, that the criteria by which some schools are judged to thrive in the competition, will be false and misleading, and that parents and the media will be inclined to assess schools on inadequate and deceptive evidence, if they study the evidence at all.

If enough people come to the conclusion that school A is better than school B, and back their judgment by sending their children to school A, they will be vindicated. School B will go out of business and school A will have all the outward signs of success.

There are obvious questions about the ability of popular schools to sustain an unplanned increase in their numbers, and the extent to which they will change (and lose their original quality) if suddenly swelled to bursting. There is no doubt that open enrolment will force local authorities to plan by attrition instead of by more rational processes of decision making. This cannot be the best way to run a railroad. But attrition will have an acceptable inevitability about it, like the Beeching cuts in railway services, if it reflects large numbers of individual choices.

Of course, that is what a market approach implies: making outcomes depend on choices by many individuals instead of a few bureaucrats. This is a matter on which the Roman Catholics, as the denomination with by far the largest share of voluntary-aided schools, feel particularly strongly.

A publication from the Catholic Bishops Conference, of which the Bishop of Leeds, Bishop David Konstant is the moving spirit, saw a threat to the Catholic character of Catholic Aided schools. Not all Aided schools have formal or effective agreements with their local authorities which guarantee them the right to restrict entry, as the first draft of the Bill (echoing the 1980 Act) seemed to assume. The Bishops foresaw an influx of non-Catholics choosing their schools because of their merits, forcing them into extra cost. Many of these fears were allayed by an amendment which allows for new agreements to be made to establish new admission limits.

But the Roman Catholics still dislike those aspects of the new regime which deprived them of the power to balance numbers between available Catholic schools in order to provide a service over a wide area. The Roman Catholics, in fact, believe they should run their schools as a complementary system, each school being developed in relation to the planned provision for all. The Act is allergic to the idea of 'systems' – it wants each school to act as a competitive individual with obligations to no one but its own pupils within the overarching requirements of the national curriculum.

Before leaving open enrolment it is important to touch briefly on the question of finance. Open enrolment means that some schools will fill and others will empty, depending on the choices which parents make. Financial delegation under the Education Reform Act, means that when a child moves from School A to School B, the budget of School B automatically benefits, and school A automatically suffers.

By laying down in law a mechanical process for ensuring that resources pass from school to school with pupils, the impact of open enrolment has been further guaranteed. It is worth remembering that open enrolment was the name used for the experiment in Kent, intended to be a pilot project for a possible voucher scheme. The idea was, within the confines of one area of a maintained school system, to maximise parents' power of choice and the corresponding ability of schools to respond. Implicit in the idea was not simply that parents should be able to choose up to the limits of existing school capacity, but beyond this, that additional classrooms should be added at popular schools to accommodate more students, if necessary.

The administrative difficulties and the inevitable costs caused that particular open enrolment experiment to lapse. The provisions of the Education Reform Act do not envisage expanding the popular schools, though this could no doubt be done at some future date without legislation. What is clear is that the combination of open enrolment and financial delegation creates a base from which it would be much easier to move forward to vouchers than it was when Sir Keith Joseph attempted to get a voucher scheme off the ground in 1981–82.

Opting Out
(Education Reform Act Chapter IV: Section 52–104– Grant-maintained schools)

The grant-maintained school proposals constitute some of the most controversial parts of the Act. Once again, the concept is extremely simple, even though it requires some 52 sections to turn it into law.

The idea is to create a new category of maintained school. Since the demise of the direct grant schools, all schools which are not maintained by local authorities have been independent schools of one kind or another. Grant-maintained schools will be financed by the Secretary of State. They will be managed by their own governing bodies and the trusts formed to own them. They will have to conform to rules which he lays down and he will have to be satisfied that they are properly run and are duly teaching the national curriculum.

The Act lays down how a school is to make the transition from being a local authority-maintained, county or voluntary school to becoming grant maintained. The decision to apply for the change of status depends on a secret postal ballot of the parents, which can be called by the governors or requisitioned by a petition from a group of parents numbering at least 20 per cent of the number of registered pupils. The voting arrangements caused much controversy. Eventually it was decided that if less than 50 per cent of parents vote, the issue is undecided and a second ballot takes place not less than fourteen days after the first result has been announced. If a simple majority of parents voting in the second ballot vote in favour of applying for grant-maintained status, the governors have six months in which to forward proposals to the DES and publish them in a prescribed form to enable objectors to submit their views to the Secretary of State.

Part of the business of putting together a proposal is to give details of the initial governing body which will take over if grant-maintained status is approved. The governors must include elected parents and teachers, but the majority must be formed by the 'first' governors (in the case of an ex-county school) and the foundation governors (in the case of an ex-voluntary school).

The legislation goes on to establish that a grant-maintained school cannot change its character – that is, change from being a comprehensive school into a grammar school, or vice versa, or change its denominational basis or its age-range, or substantially change its size – without going through the equivalent of the 'Section 12 and 13' procedures which local education authorities have to follow when they want to close or alter a school. The aim is to make it clear that a change to grant-maintained status does not imply any change to selectivity, nor is it a back door method of introducing fees. Grant-maintained schools, like all maintained schools under the Education Reform Act, are not allowed to charge admission fees.

Other sections deal with the circumstances in which grant-maintained schools may lose their grant and be discontinued, either at their own, or the Secretary of State's initiative, and how in that event the premises and property are to be disposed of.

The financial provisions aim at keeping the grant-maintained school in broadly the same financial position it would have been in had it not changed its status. The aim is that the financial clauses should be neutral. The local authority will have to pay over to the DES the per capita formula payment for pupils at the grant-maintained school which would be paid in similar circumstances to a neighbouring local authority-maintained school. Exactly how this will operate is not yet clear – for example, how far the per capita payments will be weighted for social and educational considerations like poverty and linguistic diversity. This will depend on each local authority's funding formula. Grant-maintained schools will receive somewhat larger per capita payments than county and voluntary schools because they will have to contract separately if they want to use the local authority's support services like the school psychological service, and they will have to pay for their own administration.

The grant-maintained school proposal has aroused so much hostility from within the education establishment and the local government establishment that there must be a serious risk that it will be misrepresented and misunderstood. Powerful vested interests are at work on both sides: local authorities see this in terms of the loss of schools from their sector, and think of opting out as a form of treachery and defection. Officials in the DES, on the other hand, are bound to note that this gives them, for the first time, the opportunity to have direct responsibility for a whole category of schools. For generations they have been at the receiving end of Whitehall jibes about being the last practising exponents of the late Lord Lugard's colonial principle of indirect rule. Now, after years of powerlessness and lack of executive authority over the education system for which they are theoretically responsible, at last they sense the prospect of real power and real management opportunities.

As for the teachers in the schools, their instinct is to throw in their lot with the local authorities. They are profoundly suspicious of the opting out proposal which they suspect will harm more schools than it benefits. But they have no clear idea of how it would operate or what it would really mean in practice and only a few teachers – in particular, a few headteachers – have got around to thinking seriously about how grant-maintained schools might affect them personally, for good or ill. Nor can they get very far with such speculation until the air clears and it becomes possible to consider things more dispassionately. Teachers are likely to have a good deal of influence in any school which holds a ballot on opting out. They will let parents know where they stand at an early stage: quite reasonably they will reckon their interests are directly concerned. Staff in schools which become grant maintained will have their contracts automatically transferred to the new governing body.

Let us look at the proposal under a number of convenient headings:

Timing

Before calling a ballot, governors will have to set out their case and parents will have to be given some time in which to consider it before voting. After a vote, governors are allowed six months in which to draw up their formal proposals in line with the DES rules and publish them for public examination. The Act allows two months for objections. Then, the Secretary of State must weigh the proposals and the objections. No doubt local education authorities will fight many of the proposals by concentrating attention on questions of the long-term viability of the particular school and its neighbours.

In due course the Secretary of State will give his decision to accept, reject or approve in modified form, the governors' proposals.

I think the expectation must be that relatively few grant-maintained school applications will come forward this side of 1991. The differences of emphasis between the Secretary of State and the Prime Minister on the likely take-up of grant-maintained status which became apparent at the time of the 1987 General Election, could well be simply because Mrs Thatcher has her eye on more distant horizons while Mr Baker has the immediate future in his sights. It is very difficult to see 'opting out' catching on like the sale of council houses, even if this particular parallel happens to appeal to the Prime Minister.

How easy or how difficult is it going to be to get an opting out proposal through?

The critics of the Act focused on the fact that it only takes a simple majority of those voting in the parents's secret ballot to back an application. This means that on a low poll the decision could be taken by a small minority of those affected. It is also apparent that many of those entitled to vote will no longer have children at the school by the time an application could go through, and many of those more directly affected would not be enfranchised at all, because their children would not yet have been registered.

These are valid points, and there are real doubts which must surround the preparation of an electoral list. The Act makes it the governors' responsibility to decide who is and is not a parent for the purpose of such a poll. This gets the Government off the hook, but only at the expense of impaling the governors.

Attempts to require a qualified majority, rather than a simple one, failed at the Committee stage in the Commons, but succeeded in the House of Lords only to be revised again in the House of Commons with the introduction of the requirement for a second ballot. The simple majority rule still applies.

Opinions differ on how big a hurdle it will be to get a ballot vote in favour of opting out. My own view leans towards those who think a simple majority will be far from easy to secure if there is anything like a 50 per cent poll. It will be hard enough in most governing bodies to get the two votes in favour of calling a poll, not less than four weeks apart, needed to set the procedure in motion.

Many votes are likely to be hotly contested by governors who oppose opting out and the local authorities will still have a lot of influence in governing bodies, even after they have lost their absolute majorities under the 1986 Act. Some likely candidates are obvious enough – surviving grammar schools which feel threatened by local politics are the prime candidates. In many areas it looks as if opting out will depend on an unlikely combination of brilliant undercover plotting on the one hand, and low polls and parental apathy on the other. In most schools, the activity required to whip up support for an application for grant-maintained status will, of itself, help to generate a campaign to stop it.

Even so, the situation could change if governing bodies become cockpits of political activity and parent-governor elections become politicised to a far greater degree than has happened so far; or where ethnic considerations take over and minority groups find themselves in a position to deliver blocks of votes in favour of opting out.

Ministers have suggested that they see the option to seek grant-maintained status as a safety valve for parents in deprived areas suffering as a result of ideological or educational maladministration. It has been suggested, for example, that the same formidable community feeling which has brought the John Loughborough School into being in Haringey might have been channelled into an application for grant-maintained status had this been an available option.

To suggest that the grant-maintained option will be difficult to take up in deprived areas, because of the amount of know-how and leadership required to bring a workable proposal to fruition, is to invite accusations of middle-class prejudice, and a desire to patronise groups caught in the toils of the inner city. Notwithstanding all that, I still find myself sceptical and I still believe it will not be easy to push through an opting out scheme anywhere, and particularly difficult in darkest Southwark or Tower Hamlets.

Moreover, it will in the end be the duty of the Secretary of State to vet all proposals for their viability and there is no reason to doubt that this will be done conscientiously, because nothing would damage the new grant-maintained schools more than if some inadequate proposals were approved and spectacular disasters followed.

The Secretary of State will have to look carefully at the poll and if it is small and obviously unrepresentative or ethnically split, he will have to act with great care. And he certainly could not afford to use grant-maintained status as a means of frustrating school closures if the reprieved school begins life with an inadequate school roll and no prospects. Some of the protagonists of privatisation among the New Right might be prepared to take a relaxed view of these matters and let the market decide. But this is not what the Act provides – the Act puts heavy responsibilities on the Secretary of State and there is no justification whatever for assuming that he or his successors will take them lightly.

Status

Let us now consider the status of the grant-maintained school. There has been an assumption on all sides that the grant-maintained school will acquire a status superior to that of the county school or the voluntary-aided school. I think this goes deep into the English sense of social distinctions. Ministers believe (I think) that because these new schools will not be maintained by the local authority they will be thought to be more like independent schools, run by independent boards of governors. Perhaps the hope is that some of the snobbery of the private sector will rub off on them. The question is not whether these are worthy thoughts but whether they are well founded: will the public at large accord higher status to 'opted out' schools, than to county or voluntary schools? If so, will this be because schools which already enjoy high esteem are among the first candidates for the new designation? Or will it be because, by getting more control over their own affairs they can justify a higher claim?

These are among the most difficult questions to speculate on with any confidence. Yes, I think that the English middle class would like to see a new superior category of maintained school emerge from the ruck, and if this were to happen, they would accord it higher status. Yes, I think it may well be that the first grant-maintained schools will include many which are well-established and already have good reputations which will be enhanced by a new title. Yes, I think more autonomy will enable those schools to flourish still more and in ways which benefit the pupils and staff of those schools, if not the pupils and staff elsewhere.

But it could all be very different. It has to be remembered also, that grant-maintained schools will only be funded at the levels prevailing in the local authority schools which are their neighbours. In so far as they can be compared with independent schools, many of them will have to operate a budget much smaller than those of prosperous independent prep schools or secondary schools. Budgets will vary widely from area to area. In high cost areas, like the inner cities, grant-maintained schools will be funded at levels not unlike those of private schools. In many county areas they will have little scope for self-indulgence. What the new regime will test will be the value the schools put on the support services which local authorities provide. Many schools will see no virtue in cutting themselves off from these services by opting out – or rather, they will recognise that if they want to retain those support services as an opted out school, they will have to pay for them at the point of use, and reckon the cost into their annual budgets.

Voluntary Schools
The Roman Catholics and the Anglicans find themselves

opposed to the grant-maintained school idea for general and particular reasons. They dislike the provisions because they would divide up school systems which have grown up to serve a larger area, setting school against school, and encouraging each to consider its own interest without considering the interests of others.

In particular they dislike the idea that the governors of a voluntary-aided school could opt out against the wishes of the trustees. The Roman Catholic Bishops, led by the Bishop of Leeds, expressed these doubts very cogently.

They see opting out and (as I mentioned earlier) open enrolment, as developments which must weaken the control of the diocesan authorities over the schools of their denomination and limit the diocese's ability to plan to meet the needs of all the Roman Catholic families within the area of their responsibility.

The Ministers reply that this is not correct. Trustees will continue to nominate the foundation governors which, in voluntary-aided schools and in grant-maintained schools, are in an absolute majority on the governing body. The only circumstances in which a Roman Catholic school could 'opt out' against the wishes of the trustees would be where the trustee-nominated governors defied them. The implication is that it is up to the Bishops to keep the governors in order, if necessary by sacking them, as in the case of the Archbishop of Westminster who recently sacked recalcitrants at the Cardinal Vaughan Comprehensive School in London, for stepping out of line.

For understandable reasons, the Bishops reckon this adds up to a lot of hassle which could easily be avoided by giving trustees a veto on opting out. As things stand, parents at an Aided school could requisition a vote and force an opting-out proposal through the ballot, against the wishes of the Church authorities, and the governors (a majority of whom would be nominated by the trustees who opposed the scheme) would have, by law, to submit a proposal. It would certainly be a most unedifying episode, with the Secretary of State left to arbitrate. The Bishops' objections are quite easy to understand but fairly far-fetched. And, if in extreme circumstances there were an impasse between parents, governors, and trustees of the kind envisaged in these extreme circumstances, there would be something so radically wrong that it might be no bad thing if the row sparked off a full-scale inquiry.

All this, however, does not obscure the fact that the opting-out proposals have great significance for the voluntary school authorities. Their initial reaction is hostile and they succeeded in forcing minor amendments in the House of Lords. But their attitude might well change if the arrangements survive into the 1990s. There the significant difference is the treatment of capital expenditure at grant-maintained schools and voluntary schools. The grant-maintained schools will get 100 per cent capital grants from the DES; the voluntary schools will continue to get only 85 per cent. If grant-maintained status can be made tolerable to the diocesan authorities by the conditions they lay upon their own nominated governors, it would be difficult to imagine opposition continuing indefinitely.

Most of the attention has focused so far on the implications of opting out for voluntary-aided schools, to the apparent neglect of what is going to happen to voluntary Controlled schools. The Act makes it clear that if a Controlled school opts out it will be for the trustees – in most cases this would mean the Church of England authorities – to nominate the foundation governors who would have an absolute majority on the governing body. Whereas in 1944, the Butler settlement placed them in a minority on Controlled school governing bodies, the Education Reform Act puts them back in the driver's seat. Religious education would have to follow the Agreed Syllabus, but the Church representatives would get an unexpected accession of power and influence over the running of the school – and in particular over the appointment of staff. On top of this, they would still get 100 per cent of any capital expenditure they might incur.

Special Needs

The treatment of special needs in the first draft of the Education Reform Bill was perfunctory in the extreme.Various amendments to the national curriculum sections gave headteachers greater flexibility, but specific positive policies will be needed to prevent the new Act from having the unintended effect of setting back improvements in provision.

There are obvious dangers that the combination of open enrolment, financial delegation, a national curriculum monitored by testing and assessment, and opting out, may combine to inhibit the integration of pupils with special needs within the regular school system. This goes far beyond the needs of children which are 'statemented' as the jargon has it. It will be most important that statemented children should take with them ear-marked funds to whatever school they attend, and that provision for them should be individually negotiated and monitored. But there are many children with special needs who are not covered by statements, whose presence (or absence) could be of great significance to schools in the competitive conditions which the Act aims to create. How the formulae used to distribute money to schools, build in incentives for schools to attend to special needs will be important. So will the arrangements for admissions to grant-maintained schools and whether there are pressures – intended or unintended – which discourage such schools from providing for all children, including those with learning difficulties.

Funding
I have pointed out that grant-maintained schools will be funded on more or less the same basis as their local authority-maintained neighbours. But will this be the end of the story?

Suggestions that fees might be introduced have been firmly slapped down by Mr Baker. It would certainly require primary legislation to change this. But there must be a strong expectation that grant-maintained schools would seek to raise funds from local industry and commerce, and from parents by voluntary contributions, and there will be moral pressure which will be difficult to resist.

The grant-maintained schools will have to nominate the kind of governing body that can muster strong community support, and this may well be interpreted as implying some financial commitment. Part of the change of status will be an implied readiness on the part of the school to stand on its own two feet. I suspect it will be considerably easier for a grant-maintained school to raise funds from a variety of sources than it is for most county schools. As it is, there are some exceptional county schools which have shown what can be done. They may be among the first candidates for opting out. They will certainly be the models which grant-maintained schools will be encouraged to follow.

There is also a central organisation – the Grant-Maintained Schools Trust – set up to offer advice and guidance to governors seeking to go grant maintained. Besides being an advocacy group to spread the gospel of opting out and assist in drawing up proposals, this could well develop into a representative body to promote the interests of, and raise funds for, the new category of schools.

Conclusion: The Worst and the Best

I had thought of concluding with a worst case scenario and a best case scenario. On reflection, I think it is too easy to construct the worst case – which would simply rehearse once again familiar criticisms of the Act, and lapse quickly into dark suspicions which go far beyond the present legislation. The best case scenario, on the other hand, has been underplayed because the Act has few articulate friends in the world of education.

On open enrolment, the best scenario would envisage a boost to schools which are now doing well, and a jolt to those which are most vulnerable. It would suppose that local education authorities are clever enough and imaginative enough to step in quickly with help for schools which are in trouble – and that they are left with sufficient resources at their own disposition to do so. This would imply that today there are schools which are in trouble which go largely unnoticed because their rolls are artificially sustained by zoning. Few local authorities have done what London has done and sought clearly to identify their under-performing schools. In the best case scenario, open enrolment will force local education authorities and schools to be realistic in appraising performance and applying remedies – and if necessary sanctions – to schools which are not coming up to scratch.

The best case scenario is uncomfortable and undoubtedly implies forms of competition which will be distasteful to many. But the fact is that it will merely accentuate, and force into the open, competition which is already present within the system, and if it were to force what in the new jargon must be called 'the managers' to act quickly and even ruthlessly, the result might be higher standards and greater efficiency.

A critical element in the Act – exemplified both by open enrolment and opting out – is the reduced role for the local education authority. The role of the local politicians is undoubtedly going to be curbed, and confined largely to budget making and the levying of a community charge. But, shorn of many administrative tasks in the running of schools, the local education authority (in the persons of its education officers, advisers and inspectors) will be in a position to devote a much greater share of their time and energy to monitoring the system, directing support services, in-service training and curriculum development activities, and carrying out the remedial and disciplinary tasks arising from the new emphasis on quality and performance.

As to grant-maintained schools, here, it seems to me, the best case scenario depends on an acceptance of the philosophy behind the proposals. In other words, the grant-maintained schools are part of a larger pattern of social reform of which education is only an incidental part.

The pattern is essentially that of an atomised school system – a set of separate, individual units, each trying according to its own methods and models, to take a national curriculum and teach it in the most effective way. It is a competitive system, because (so the argument runs) all institutions operating in parallel must be made to compete or else they become slack and complacent. It accepts the reality of pecking orders and builds upon it – because pecking orders are there, whether we recognise them or not, and high standards are achieved by letting this come out into the open rather than pretending to a non-existent equality.

Mr Baker has commented frequently on the monotony of the education system as set up at present – a small independent sector embracing 7 per cent of the population, and all the other 93 per cent in a maintained system. He wants to introduce half-way houses and intermediate systems of free education, so that there are other targets to aim at, other schools to choose, besides the local authority-maintained schools. Grant-maintained schools in this reckoning, might come to absorb, say, 20 per cent of the system. City technology colleges might take in another 3 or 4 per cent, if, again in the 1990s, they received a boost. This would dent, but not eliminate the county and voluntary school network, reducing it to, say, 65–70 per cent of the whole.

The result would be a much more varied system, held together by a national curriculum and national external examinations. And, because it would be a more varied system, it would be more susceptible to parental demands – more eager to satisfy parents' wishes and expectations, less subject to the conspiracy of the professionals whose instinct is to bend the educational process to their own convenience and interests.

After a while – so runs this optimistic scenario – people would get so used to such a system that they would barely recall the bad old days before the Education Reform Act. Even the educational establishment would come round, in time, and because of its incorrigibly conservative character, become as attached to the new structure as it had once been to the old.

Certainly, this scenario envisages a hierarchy of institutions, and in time an unofficial system of selection based upon it: not selection like the 11+, but selection by emergence which would produce specialised institutions and discourage pupils from taking courses they couldn't cope with while enabling the highflyers to go foward without impediment.

A scenario like this would make a lot of sense in the 1990s if the Thatcher revolution continues and the hoped-for destruction of the dependency culture is achieved. A competitive education system, in which institutions, no less than individuals, find themselves permanently engaged in struggles for promotion and relegation, might be the natural counterpart to the enterprise culture and the world beyond the welfare state. It would complete the repudiation of R.A. Butler's social reforming aims for the education system: where he saw the object of educational reform as the creation of social harmony and social cohesion, the enterprise culture would substitute aims of self-reliance, competition and wealth creation. It would reward effort and punish idleness – it would be unflinching in its recognition that children have to bear the consequences of their parent's choices. By forcing decisions back to parents, it would reward those who support their children and penalise those who fail to do so, justifying this on grounds of earthy realism, and a kind of ruthless Darwinian morality.

A country which decided to support this kind of an educational system would, by definition, have travelled quite a long way further down the Thatcherite road – and Mrs Thatcher, herself, is a realistic and cautious politician who has not achieved what she has over the past decade by pressing her ideology to absurd limits.

Much more likely, and in many ways worse, is the prospect of further, piece-meal reform. Grant-maintained schools, if they prove to be a less than spectacular success, may have the path cleared for them, by improving the financial terms and allowing independent schools to 'opt in', or by easing the way for more selective entry. If I were Mr Baker, I would be looking at the techniques now being proposed for taking inner-city housing out of local authority hands and handing it over to mini-development boards: why not do the same for inner city education? Opting out could take on a whole new meaning. And if new agencies were created for the purpose it would be much easier to channel money and resources, directly to the worst areas, without pouring it into the treacle mine of Rate Support Grant.

All this takes us a long way beyond my immediate remit for which I apologise, but as I noted at the beginning, the Act is far-reaching and will affect the education system in future years, in ways which have not yet been thought of. Whether it is right to call it an Education Reform Act is a matter on which everyone is entitled to an opinion. What is beyond doubt is that nothing will be the same again now that it has been passed.

References

Education Act (1902) HMSO
Education Act (1944) HMSO
Education Act (1980) HMSO
Education Act (1986) HMSO
Education Act (1988) HMSO

2

The National Curriculum

Denis Lawton

Introduction

My task is to discuss those parts of the Education Reform Act which refer to the national curriculum. I will try to confine myself to that, although the national curriculum is clearly part of a much more general picture, and it is difficult to separate some aspects of the national curriculum from other sections of the Act, such as the opting out clauses, which have been analysed by Stuart Maclure in Chapter 1. It will also be necessary to see the national curriculum and the proposals for national testing as complementary, but I will avoid going over the ground which Desmond Nuttall will cover in Chapter 3.

Arguments in Favour of a National Curriculum

First of all I would like to make it clear that I am not opposed to the idea of a national curriculum; many, perhaps most, curriculum specialists now share general approval for the principle of a national curriculum, whilst disliking some particular features of the version contained in the Education Reform Act.

The following arguments have been put forward from time to time in favour of a national curriculum:

1   All children should have a right of access to a worthwhile curriculum.
2   There ought to be as much consensus as possible nationally on the general aims and objectives of compulsory education.
3   An egalitarian view which stresses equalising access to

educational chances on a national basis, reducing local differences in quality of education offered.
4   Common schools should transmit a common culture by means of a common curriculum.
5   That it is important for all schools to share common standards which will ensure reasonable levels of teacher expectation.
6   That a national curriculum facilitates the geographic mobility of pupils.
7   A national curriculum increases the accountability of schools.

Not all of these are arguments which Mr Baker would use: only the last three were stressed in the Consultation Document (DES 1987d); the kind of national curriculum which is advocated will tend to vary according to the reasons put forward to support it. In other words, we should be talking about *a* national curriculum rather than *the* national curriculum.

The Background: Steps Towards a National Curriculum in 1987

On 9 January 1987, Mr Baker made a speech to the North of England Conference on Education, in Rotherham. (DES 1987a). He began by mentioning England's 'eccentric' educational system – less centralised and standardised than, for example, France or Germany. He also argued that existing standards were not high enough, and complained about the lack of agreement concerning the 14–16 age group's curriculum, stressing the confusion in schools over the question of balance, and the failure to work out satisfactory objectives:

'These weaknesses do not arise in those West European countries where the schools follow more or less standard national syllabuses. In those countries the school system produces results which overall are at least as satisfactory as those produced here; and the teachers are no less professional than ours. Nor do these countries show any sign of wanting to give up the advantages of national syllabuses. So it would be foolish to reject out of hand the idea of moving much nearer to the kind of curricular structure which obtains elsewhere in Western Europe. For my part, I am sure that we must so move . . .'

When politicians make international comparisons to support their arguments on education, they tend to be very selective in their choice of examples. This is no exception. Mr Baker ignored the fact that many West European countries with centralised curricula are trying very hard to free schools from too much central control. There are advantages and disadvantages in having a centralised system.

Nevertheless, similar arguments in favour of a national curriculum were repeated and developed throughout 1987. Later in January, Mr Baker made a speech to the Society of Education Officers (DES 1987b); in April he outlined his proposals to the Education, Science and Arts Committee of the House of Commons (DES 1987c) and they became an important part of the Conservative election programme. After the election, the Consultation Document on *The National Curriculum 5 to 16* was published in July 1987, and in his Manchester speech (September, DES 1987e) Mr Baker elaborated on the proposals which were later included in the Education Reform Act.

The proposed national curriculum has four components:

1 *Subjects:* English, maths and science are designated *core* subjects; technology, history, geography, music, art, physical education, and a modern foreign language are *foundation* subjects; the core and foundation subjects will take up 70–80 per cent of the timetable, but specific time allocations for each subject are not included in the legislation.

2 *Attainment targets*, which are defined as 'clear objectives for the knowledge, skills, understanding and aptitudes which pupils of different abilities and maturity should be expected to have acquired at or near certain ages'.

3 *Programmes of study*, defined as 'describing the essential content which needs to be covered to enable pupils to reach or surpass the attainment targets'.

4 *An assessment programme* at 7, 11, 14 and 16.

Criticisms of the Baker Version of a National Curriculum
Given the general support for a national curriculum, why then
has Mr Baker's national curriculum been widely criticised?

1   It gives the appearance of being a bureaucratic document,
seemingly concerned with controlling the timetable rather than
improving the quality of teaching and learning experiences.

2   The curriculum structure which is proposed is obsolete,
neglecting important areas of learning such as political
awareness, economic understanding, health education and
moral development. (The document *Education Reform* states that
the national curriculum is set in 'a clear moral framework', but
this is mere rhetoric unless it means the morality of the market
place!).

3   It seems to be more concerned with market forces (parental
choice) than with curriculum planning.

4   Teachers are not central to this curriculum and appear to be
regarded as routine workers transmitting central syllabuses
rather than sharing 'ownership' of the curriculum.

5   The national curriculum will not apply to independent
schools – it may, therefore, be seen as inferior to what is offered
in independent schools, reinforcing the suspicion that it is a
device for accountability and control of teachers.

6   Little thought seems to have been given to the provision of
adequate numbers of specialist teachers for the new curriculum.
There will be serious shortages of teachers of mathematics,
science and modern languages as well as technology. This lack
of forethought is symptomatic of a technicist attitude to
curriculum – regarding the provision of time and syllabuses as
more important than good teachers.

All of these are serious criticisms, but perhaps the most
important is that Mr Baker has, in preferring this model, ignored
the lessons that could have been learned from the last forty years
of educational development. What are some of the important
lessons which might have been learned?

1   Psychologists now regard with great suspicion the ideas

which encouraged the rigid categorisation of children into three kinds of ability with different kinds of schools or curricula. The worst aspects of that view may have been avoided in the present Act, but they are not entirely absent – how else can we explain city technology colleges, for example? Similarly, psychologists no longer think about intellectual development in terms of fixed, age-related norms. Yet benchmark testing at 7, 11, 14 and 16 was an important feature of the original curriculum proposals, and it is still not clear to what extent Professor Black's TGAT proposals will eliminate that danger. (See below.)

We have also learned to be very suspicious of the behavioural objectives, training model of curriculum planning which deprofessionalises the teachers and trivialises the educational process, but there is plenty of evidence of that kind of obsolete thinking in the Act: for example, age-related achievement targets. The curriculum seems to be thought of mainly in terms of packages of information to be mastered.

2   Philosophers all over the world – not least here at the Institute of Education – have moved far beyond school subjects as a basis of categorising knowledge: Philip Phenix (1964) in the USA talked of *Realms of Meaning*, Hirst and Peters (1978) wrote extensively about the 'forms of knowledge'. John White (1973) wrote a book about compulsory curriculum which Sir Keith Joseph read but failed to understand. Malcolm Skilbeck, before becoming our Professor of Curriculum Studies, devised, as head of the Curriculum Development Centre, a *Core Curriculum for Australian Schools* (1980) in which he stated clearly the relationship between subjects and curriculum planning:

> 'Merely to define the core curriculum as a set of compulsory subjects is, however, unsatisfactory. To simply list the subjects is to miss one vital requirement of core curriculum, namely, that subject matter, teaching, learning processes and learning situations, should be organised around a set of aims, principles and values, which relate to the defined characteristics and major needs of contemporary society and all youth.' (p. 13)

3   Sociologists and anthropologists have also successfully questioned the cultural assumptions made, or taken for granted, by the traditional school curriculum, as well as its implications for various social groups in modern industrial, multicultural communities. Sociologists, notably Professor Bernstein, have challenged the traditional, liberal-humanist view of education which suggests that the state promotes educational policies which are in the general public interest and for the general good, and that if individuals fail to take advantage of the curriculum offered in this neutral distribution process, than it is somehow their fault. All of this work is completely ignored.

In the Baker version of the national curriculum, there is much talk of balance. But what we are now offered is not a balanced diet, but a kind of anti-scurvy curriculum: we have a list of ingredients that Mr Baker thinks will be good for us, without any justification for the list. This is not a balanced diet prepared by a nutritionist based on scientific theory, but a quack doctor's list of prejudices with unexplained percentages attached as the recommended dosage for each item. Mr Baker seems to be saying 'eat plenty of lemons' whilst knowing nothing about ascorbic acid. If he wants to prescribe a balanced diet for all children he should be identifying the equivalent curriculum terms to vitamins, proteins, carbohydrates and minerals. We will need much more than a list of subject ingredients to convince us. Before going on to prescribe these subjects in even greater detail he should at least see whether there are more satisfactory models available than a list of subjects which are disturbingly similar to the 1904 Secondary Regulations:

> 'English Language and Literature (not less than 4½ hours)
> Geography and History (not less than 4½ hours)
> Languages, ancient and modern (3½ hours)
> Mathematics and Science (7½ hours)
> The curriculum should also contain physical exercise, drawing and singing.'

In his Manchester, 1987 speech, Mr Baker attempted to answer criticisms of his subject curriculum but, although it is one of his best speeches on curriculum, he sadly missed the major point.

He spent much time saying that surely we could not have a curriculum without mathematics or science or history . . . Of course he is right in that but, without some theoretical basis to the curriculum, such as that suggested by Malcolm Skilbeck, there will be no guidance on *what kind of* mathematics and science should be included for all children. And as Dearden (1981) pointed out in his analysis of an earlier version of the national curriculum, you cannot talk sensibly about a balanced curriculum without specifying your prior commitment to whatever it is you wish to balance. Subjects may be useful as means to curriculum ends, but they are not ends in themselves. This is the fundamental error of the curriculum based on subjects. By all means use subjects, but we need to know what we are using them for.

Bureaucratic and Professional Attitudes to Education

So, why did Mr Baker choose such an unsatisfactory model? One possible answer is that Mr Baker really does think of the curriculum as subjects in a common sense way; a second explanation is that he sees a simple subject curriculum as what most parents would like – a reassurance that their children are being offered real maths and English etc. Either or both of these explanations – the common sense and the populist – may be right, but there are also more complex explanations which may be even more significant.

It is possible to identify two sets of attitudes towards the education service in England and Wales – the bureaucratic and the professional. Bureaucrats are concerned with the efficiency of the whole system and need statistical information to demonstrate that efficiency. Professionals, however, should be concerned with the quality of the teaching process and the needs of individual children. The bureaucratic approach concentrates on output and testing, whereas professionals focus on the quality of input and the skills, knowledge and awareness of the teacher. The bureaucratic approach is associated with norms, benchmarks, average performance and norm-related data, whereas the professional approach concentrates on individual differences, the learning process and criterion referencing. The bureaucratic curriculum is based on traditional subjects; the professional curriculum treats subjects as a means of achieving higher level aims. Members of Her Majesty's Inspectorate, for example, have described how subjects may be used to achieve coverage of a list of 'Areas of Learning and Experience' (DES/HMI, 1977).

It is always dangerous and misleading to contrast two sets of attitudes in this way: it is tempting to see the dichotomy as a conflict between good and evil, heroes and villains. But reality is more complicated than that. The point I am trying to make is that the bureaucrats have a perfectly legitimate right to be concerned about 'efficiency'; it is part of their job to ensure 'value for money' by means of accountability processes; they need 'performance indicators'. But it is possible for policy-makers to become excessively concerned with 'efficiency' and to lose sight of the real purpose of the enterprise. So, having stressed the legitimate concern of bureaucrats with efficiency, it is also necessary to say that if the bureaucrats win too much influence at the expense of the professionals, then there may be serious dangers of curriculum distortion.

Why should this happen? One reason will be that from time to time a natural affinity may develop between bureaucrats and the politicians in power. In this context it is important to observe that the DES is not a simple tug of war between professionals and bureaucrats but a complex tension system involving politicians as well. There will be occasions when the dominant political attitudes to education will encourage bureaucrats to exert more power, control and influence than may be healthy.

Some, but not all, current political attitudes facilitate bureaucratic control. Another word of caution: we should not read policy documents as evidence of what politicians intend, but as examples of prevailing values and ideologies. And we should read their speeches as well as the official documents. It may be a mistake to ask what Mr Baker, or anyone else, 'intended' by the Consultation Document (DES 1987d) or the Act. These texts may be more usefully analysed as expressions of ideology rather than as clearly thought-out plans or intentions. And we should not be surprised by inconsistencies, or even contradictions. There is no one clear-cut Conservative set of values and beliefs on education.

I have elsewhere (1988) suggested that it is useful to think of four ideological positions on education within the current political context:

1 The privatisers
2 The minimalists or segregators
3 The pluralists
4 The comprehensive planners

1 The Privatisers
The 'pure' version of this view recommends privatising all education, from pre-school provision to university. Local education authorities would be disbanded, all schools would be run by boards of governors or by private companies. Parents would have complete freedom to choose – moderated only by their ability to pay. The ideological background to this view is *laissez-faire* capitalism with total reliance on market mechanisms to control the relation between supply and demand in education. 'Choice' is the key concept.

Some of you may doubt whether total privatisers still exist. If so, note the following:

> 'The blind, unplanned, uncoordinated wisdom of the market . . . is overwhelmingly superior to the well-researched, rational, systematic, well meaning, cooperative, science-based, forward-looking, statistically respectable plans of governments . . . The market system is the greatest generator of national wealth known to mankind: coordinating and fulfilling the diverse needs of countless individuals in a way which no human mind or minds could ever comprehend, without coercion, without direction, without bureaucratic interference.'
> (K. Joseph, 'Stranded on the Middle Ground' 1976, quoted by George and Wilding in *Ideology and Social Welfare*, 1985, p.27)

Sir Keith Joseph was at heart a privatiser, but when he became Secretary of State for Education, he was persuaded by his civil servants to adopt a more politically acceptable stance. A difficulty about this category of privatisers is that it is not easy to find examples in a 'pure' form; privatisers tend to 'water down' their public utterances. Nevertheless, the ideology is very important as a strand of Conservative thinking on education and as an influence on policy. As recently as 6 August 1987, Sir Alfred Sherman, who had been an influential policy adviser to the Conservative Party, wrote an article in the *Daily Telegraph* advocating the privatisation of all schools. The title is intriguing: 'How Everyone Could Have a Public School Education' – there is an assumption there that someone should have challenged . . . and Oliver Letwin (1988) who has been political adviser on education to both Sir Keith Joseph and Mrs Thatcher, has recently written a book with the intriguing title *Privatising the World*.

Privatisers would not be in favour of any kind of national curriculum. But their views may not be unimportant in determining the form of the national curriculum which has been chosen.

2   The Minimalists

Minimalists believe in a mixed economy in education. The state should provide basic schooling (as cheaply as possible) and parents should be able to buy additional extras or to opt out of the state system altogether. This attitude has led to what Tawney (1921) criticised as a system run by those who felt that it was not good enough for their own children. Some voucher systems could operate within this scenario, for example, that advocated by Stuart Sexton (1987). The Assisted Places Scheme is also characteristic of the thinking behind minimalism, by signalling clearly that state schools are not really good enough for bright children. Mr Baker's city technology colleges represent another example of this' approach. And good schools will be encouraged to opt out of the LEA system in order to offer something better to discriminating parents.

Minimalists also tend to be segregators; they want to separate children according to social class, or supposed intellectual ability, perhaps by sex. Minimalists are not in favour of a common curriculum, but they may advocate a low level basic national curriculum enforced by tests. Parents will be encouraged to choose, and therefore must be provided with evidence on which to make rational choices – thus national testing programmes are essential for the provision of league tables of good and bad schools.

3   *The Pluralists*

Pluralists would like a state system that is so good that there would be little or no incentive to use independent schools, but many of them doubt whether such an ideal is attainable, and their regard for individual freedom of choice would not allow them to legislate private schools out of existence. Freedom to choose is, for the pluralists, more important than social justice. Pluralists invented such terms as 'parity of esteem' (for the different but equal types of secondary school within the tripartite system). They tend to meritocratic beliefs in education, favouring the metaphor of 'the ladder of opportunity'. Some pluralists are uneasy about the idea of a common curriculum, because they doubt the capacity of those of 'lower ability' to follow a worthwhile common curriculum. In the past they tended to advocate the now discredited 'core plus options' curriculum, and have not yet found a replacement for it. Some Tory politicians might be included in this category – Butler and Boyle, possibly, and from the evidence of his speech in the House of Commons on 1 December 1987, Ted Heath.

4   *The Comprehensive Planners*

'Comprehensive planners' refers to those who want to change the secondary curriculum to adjust to the needs of mass education. They tend to criticise the grammar school curriculum for a variety of reasons – epistemological, cultural and social as well as political (Lawton, 1983). Their attempts to devise a common curriculum rest on ideological assumptions about common culture and common schools without denying individual differences and the need to provide for individual opportunities within a common plan.

   Comprehensive planners will generally be in favour of centralised planning and the professionalism of teachers; access to curriculum must be completely open – the aim is a good general education for all ('the broad highway' metaphor). There may be some Conservative MPs in this goup, but if so, they kept quiet during the debate on the Education Reform Act. It is certainly not part of mainstream Conservative thinking.

Which National Curriculum?

Thus, privatisers would have nothing to do with any kind of national curriculum: it would be completely contrary to the dominance of market choice. The other three groups might appear to be talking about a national curriculum, but what they really mean by that term is very different in each case. For many years some comprehensive schools have been trying to develop a common curriculum, but the Baker proposal for a national curriculum is not a radical step in that direction; it is a retreat away from the ideals of comprehemsive education to a minimalist position, with a few concessions to pluralist thinking, but even more concessions to the privatisers' market ideology. This national curriculum has to be seen along with the earlier Conservative proposals for the Assisted Places Scheme, the opting out facilities, and the fact that Mr Baker has refused to make the national curriculum compulsory for independent schools.

A dominant belief behind the Act is the market; choice is the acceptable face of market ideology. And in order to choose rationally parents must have evidence on which to base their choice. This evidence will be provided by test results converted into league tables. From this analysis it would be wrong to see the tests as a way of reinforcing the national curriculum; it would be more credible to see the national curriculum as a crude framework for the testing programme. From a political point of view, league tables are much more important than the national curriculum itself. I do not suggest that that is the whole truth, but I do think it is an important part of it. The other important part of the truth may be to see the national curriculum as a means of accountability and control. In both cases the curriculum is subordinated to other more important political priorities. Hence the completely non-professional presentation of the national curriculum. And neither the curriculum nor the assessment programme will apply to independent schools where the market has other ways of operating, unless, of course, those schools see that it is in their interests to play the assessment game and turn it to their advantage.

Testing or Assessment?

If I stopped at this point the picture would be a very gloomy one. But there may be a little light at the end of the tunnel. One of the aspects of the national curriculum which has been much criticised is national testing at 7, 11, 14 and 16. Many critics felt that the proposed testing was even more dangerous than the national curriculum. But the complex operation of producing an assessment and testing programme was entrusted to Professor Paul Black and a small Task Group on Assessment and Testing (TGAT). Their Report was published in January 1988 (DES 1988a). If their proposals are fully implemented the assessment procedures could improve the national curriculum. I cannot hope to summarise the whole of the report of the Task Group on Assessment and Testing here, but I would like to touch on some of the reasons for my optimism. They are all connected with the fact that assessment is seen by Professor Black and his colleagues as an integral part of the teaching-learning process. The TGAT Report recommends that:

1 Assessment will be age-related but the standards will not be. The concept of 'progression' is very important and this is to be indicated by ten levels of pupil achievement which are deliberately not age-related. From a curriculum point of view this is very important.

2 At age 7 there will be an assessment procedure including formative tests designed to identify whether the pupils are achieving at levels 1, 2 or 3. If a 7-year-old pupil is performing at level 1, he may need some special remedial attention with perhaps more detailed diagnostic testing to identify the needs more precisely; similarly, if he or she is already at level 3, that pupil may need to be given special opportunities to continue to make advances within that subject. The major features of assessment at 7 is that the tasks will be formative and criterion referenced. Teachers will be able to choose some Standard Assessment Tasks (SATs) from a national item bank, hence ensuring comparability of standards. What we know about curriculum implementation would strongly support the idea of

teachers choosing from nationally agreed materials.

3   The next reporting stage will take place four years later at age 11 at the end of primary education, but meanwhile, pupils will be expected to progress by one broadly defined level every two years – the avoidance of a one-year, one-level relationship will make possible curriculum differentiation of a kind much more flexible than streaming, and will avoid a scheme which would be too detailed.

4   At age 11 and 14, teachers will choose what level of achievement it will be most appropriate to assess each child in for each subject (hence there will be no general statement that pupil 'x' is at level 4.) Also, at each level the aggregated score for a subject will be less important than the profile of pupil achievement which will show three of four different components in each subject (e.g. in English: reading, writing, speaking, listening). Teachers will record both the aggregated mark (which will be important bureaucratically) as well as the individual profiles which will be of much greater curriculum value. It is not much use knowing that a pupil scored 55 per cent, but it is very helpful to have details of strengths and weaknesses.

5   At age 11 (and 14) the spread of achievement will be much wider than the three-level range expected at age 7. This would seem to imply a greater repertoire of teaching techniques together with an ability to diagnose difficulties. Standardised tests will only do part of this job for the teacher.

6   In the secondary school one implication may be a more flexible curriculum structure which will allow pupils to progress at different rates. Setting or streaming would be much less suitable than something like the vertical timetabling now in operation in Western Australia. This would give real choice for pupils rather than spurious choice, but the choice would be constrained by previous achievements.

We are warned by Professor Black and his colleagues that an ambitious programme of assessment and testing of this kind will require a substantial investment of time (particularly teacher time) and other resources. Adequate resources including in-service programmes for the teachers will be necessary, and the form of assessment will place at a premium cooperation within and between schools. It will need several years to develop the assessment programme after the curriculum has been established.

What we could have here is a very interesting attempt to bridge the gap between bureaucratic and professional concerns. But it will be important for the whole Report to be accepted if it is to achieve professional goals. The danger may be that it will be regarded as much too complicated to implement. The alternative of age-related standardised tests would, however, be completely disastrous.

Summary
1   There is much support for the principle of a national curriculum.
2   Because of this support the opposition to the national curriculum may appear to be confused and inconsistent.
3   The distinction between bureaucratic and professional attitudes is not generally understood.
4   The influence of political ideology is equally unclear and hence there is an apparent convergence of bureaucratic and political values. But there is no one single Conservative ideology in education.
5   Testing is often seen as a bureaucratic device exerting an undesirable influence on the curriculum, but assessment is not necessarily bureaucratic: 'Promoting children's learning is a principal aim of schools. Assessment lies at the heart of this process . . .' (TGAT Report).

Conclusion

Many of us argued against Mr Baker's version of a national curriculum whilst the Bill was being debated. But now the Bill has become an Act and this national curriculum is a legal requirement it is the duty of teachers and other educationists to make the best of it and to work towards its implementation and gradual improvement.

There is still much to be gained from a national curriculum, even one which is imperfectly designed. After all, most schools now use a list of subjects as a basis for achieving curricular objectives, and will not find the list required by the 1988 Act particularly objectionable. Moreover, the Act does not specify how the curriculum is to be delivered nor what teaching methods should be used. Teachers will have opportunities at school level to plan how best to overcome the limitations of a curriculum defined in terms of subjects.

Similarly, those involved in the various subject working groups, charged by the Secretary of State with the task of giving guidance on attainment targets and programmes of study, will have opportunities for establishing links between subjects, and for cooperating on cross-curricular themes.

It will be necessary to continue to protest about the theoretical inadequacy of this national curriculum as well as the practical problems involved. Mr Baker has promised us that 'the National Curriculum Council will have a continuing remit – after the system has been launched – to keep programmes of study and assessment instruments under review. In this way constructive change will actually be encouraged' (Baker, DES 1987e). We must make the most of these long-term opportunities. The present version of a national curriculum is a missed opportunity but it need not be seen as an educational disaster.

References

Dearden, R. F. (1981) 'Balance and Coherence' *Cambridge Journal of Education*, Vol. II, No. 2.

Department of Education and Science (1977) *Curriculum 11–16* (HMI Red Book One). London: HMSO.

Department of Education and Science (1987a) Secretary of State's Rotherham Speech 'Kenneth Baker looks at the future of the Education System'. Press Release 11/87 (9th January).

Department of Education and Science (1987b) 'Kenneth Baker calls for curriculum for pupils of all abilities'. Press Release 22/87 (23rd January).

Department of Education and Science (1987c) 'Secretary of State's Statement announcing Working Groups on Mathematics and Science to the Education, Science and Arts Select Committee'. Press Release (7th April).

Department of Education and Science and Welsh Office (1987d) *The National Curriculum 5–16: a consultation document.* London: DES (July).

Department of Education and Science (1987e) Secretary of State's Manchester Speech 'National Curriculum is the key to better standards . . .'

Press Release (September).

Department of Education and Science (1987f) Education Reform: Government Proposals for Schools. London: DES pamphlet (December).

Department of Education and Science (1988a) *National Curriculum: Task Group on Assessment and Testing: A Report. London: DES (January).*

Department of Education and Science (1988b) National Curriculum TGAT: Three Supplementary Reports. London: DES (December).

George, V. and Wilding, P. (1985) *Ideology and Social Welfare.*London: Routledge and Kegan Paul.

Heath, E. House of Commons Speech (1 December 1987). Official Report of House of Commons Parliamentary Debates. London: Hansard.

Hirst, P. H. and Peters, R. S. (1970) *The Logic of Education.* London: Routledge and Kegan Paul.

Joseph, Sir K. (1976) *Stranded on the Middle Ground.* London: Centre for Policy Studies.

Lawton, D. (1983) *Curriculum Studies and Educational Planning.* London: Hodder and Stoughton.

Lawton, D. (1988) 'Ideologies of Education' in Lawton, D. and Chitty, C. (eds.) *The National Curriculum*, Bedford Way Papers/33. London: Institute of Education, University of London.

Letwin, O. (1988) *Privatising the World.* London: Cassell.

Phenix, P. H. (1964) *Realms of Meaning.* London: McGraw-Hill.

Sexton, S. (1987) *Our Schools: A Radical Policy.* London: Institute of Economic Affairs.

Sherman, Sir Alfred (1987) 'How Everyone could have a Public School Education'. London: *Daily Telegraph* (6 August).

Skilbeck, M. (1980) *A Core Curriculum for Australian Schools.* Canberra: Curriculum Development Council.

Tawney, R. H. (1921) *The Acquisitive Society.* London: Bell and Sons.

White, J. P. (1973) *Towards a Compulsory Curriculum.* London: Routledge and Kegan Paul.

Whitty, G. *et al.* (1986) 'Assisting Whom? Benefits and Costs of the Assisted Places Scheme', *British Educational Research Journal.* Conference Paper. Oxfordshire, Abingdon: Carfax Publishing Company.

3

National Assessment: Complacency or Misinterpretation?

Desmond Nuttall

In the first chapter, Stuart Maclure called the Education Reform Act 'the most far-reaching and important piece of education legislation since 1944'. Many, like me, feel uneasy about the underlying philosophy of the Act; it is designed to encourage competition between schools and implicitly between pupils, and to reduce the power of the local education authorities. In this chapter I will be addressing the topic of national assessment, a topic which is not covered in any great detail in the Act. Indeed there are only one or two passing references in the context of the provisions for the national curriculum. In particular, Section 4 says that:

> 'The Secretary of State may, by orders, specify in relation to each of the foundation subjects such attainment targets, such programmes of study and such assessment arrangements as he considers appropriate for that subject.'

– and that's about it on national assessment. Later sections of the Act give the details of the constitution of the School Examinations and Assessment Council (SEAC) but say little of its duties. It is noticeable that there is no requirement upon SEAC to consult, though in contrast the National Curriculum Council does have to consult about the nature of the curriculum proposals.

Thus, we cannot look to the Act itself to find out how the assessment system will work; we must look to the Report of the Task Group on Assessment and Testing (TGAT)[1]. In this chapter I want to examine the TGAT proposals critically; but here I face a dilemma. On the one hand I am very unhappy about the underlying philosophy not only of the Act but also of an elaborate and untried system of national assessment in up to ten subjects of the curriculum at four different ages. I am also very critical of the negligible amount of time for consultation over the proposals. Nor would I find it difficult to find fault with a number of the arguments put forward in the Report. Moreover, like the leader writer of *The Times*, I am somewhat suspicious of the reaction to the Report: he or she wrote:

> 'Something curious is surely happening in the education world when the big teacher unions and the Labour Party joined Mr Kenneth Baker in welcoming a report that shows exactly how children can be tested at the ages of 7, 11, 14 and 16.'[2]

On the other hand, I have a feeling that being a whingeing academic does not help in the present climate. The Government wants national assessment, parents want national assessment;[3] they have become very impatient with education professionals who bring up nothing but objections and difficulties. We are going to get national assessment and the TGAT proposals are not as oppressive and anti-educational as many feared. Paul Black himself said at a BERA Conference that:

> 'It is easy enough to construct as an Aunt Sally some simplistic and oppressive alternatives and then to show the virtues of the TGAT Report by comparison – perhaps the Report received more than its deserved share of welcome by this very process.'[4]

We must recognise that Mr Baker is under pressure from the Prime Minister and the right wing of the Conservative Party to adopt a much simpler and tougher method of testing, but it does seem that by publication of the summary of the TGAT proposals[5] the Secretary of State, in the words of *Education*, 'has won a significant victory over his right wing critics' and further that 'Mr Baker's approval of the DES propaganda mission is being viewed as a sign of his unconditional endorsement of the Report'.[6] So the political realities suggest that, at the present time, if one destroys the TGAT proposals one is more likely to find in their place a more oppressive system; if on the other hand one largely accepts them, and seeks ways of improving and implementing them sensitively, one is likely to arrive at the least bad solution. So I take the view that the balance of advantage lies in being constructively critical about the Report – a report that offers the best set of national assessment proposals that we are likely to get.

What I would like to do is to evaluate them against the background of my own appreciation of current initiatives to improve assessment (Figure 1), and TGAT's own criteria (Figure 2). The key words are *criterion-referenced, formative, moderated* and *relating to progression*.

Current initiatives are striving to make assessment

- more comprehensive
- provide better and quicker feedback
- more positive
- give more responsibility to the student
- create flexibility and adaptability in the student
- more valid

Figure 1

The Four Criteria

- The assessment results should give direct information about pupils' achievement in relation to objectives: they should be *criterion-referenced;*
- The results should provide a basis for decisions about pupils' further learning needs: they should be *formative;*
- The scale or grades should be capable of comparison across classes and schools, if teachers and parents are to share a common language and common standards: so the assessments should be *calibrated* or *moderated*:
- The ways in which criteria and scales are set up and used should relate to expected routes of educational development, giving some continuity to a pupil's assessment at different ages: the assessments should *relate to progression*.

Figure 2

The essence of the proposals is that the attainment targets should be clustered into ten levels spanning the age range 7–16. The norm would be progress by one level every two years, as Figure 3 shows. At age 7 one would expect that most pupils would achieve either level 1, 2 or 3; level 2 being the expected level, and level 1 indicating that a student might need considerable extra help.

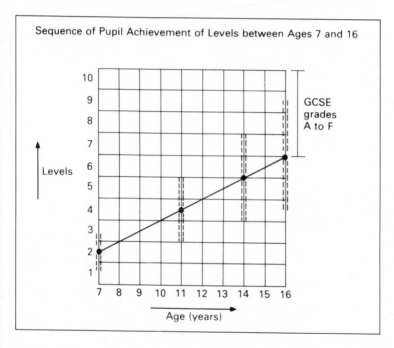

Figure 3

These levels are designed to apply not to subjects as a whole but to a number of profile components within each subject. A profile component is a cluster of related attainment targets that have some intellectual coherence (though it is likely that different principles will be used to devise the profile components in different subjects – incidentally they were called domains when similar work was being done for the GCSE). The

TGAT proposal is that each subject should comprise up to *six* profile components by the age of 16, though as Figure 4 shows they are expecting some profile components to emerge by a process either of bifurcation or by insertion, so that at age 7 there will not be nearly as many profile components within a subject as there will be by the age of 16. Indeed one could expect up to *forty* profile components by the age of 16 on the assumption that there are seven subjects that are going to be defined in terms of attainment targets, while art, music and PE will simply have guidelines.

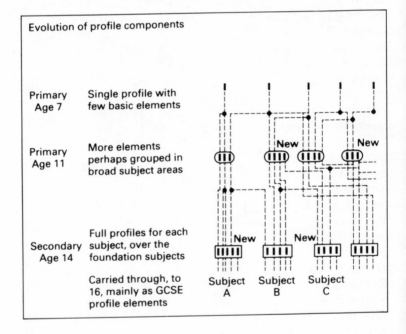

Figure 4

The assessment will actually be done by a combination of assessment by teachers and nationally standardised assessment tasks. The teachers' assessment will be moderated by groups of teachers who meet to discuss the work of students on the standardised tasks and their own assessments. For 7-year-olds the proposals are, I think, very sensitive: the assessment tasks are to be as naturalistic as possible, that is, part of the normal work in the classroom rather than specially set-up situations. Tasks or assignments should be chosen by teachers from a bank that will allow the assessment of a wide range of diverse skills, so that instead of having a test for English, a test for maths, and a test for science there will be tasks which should allow the assessment of attainment targets and profile components covering maths, English and science. One of the examples given in the Report is of 'winter through to spring': language work comes from discussing the question 'how do we keep warm in the winter?' For maths there could be a survey of the clothes worn by children in the classroom, and later some science experiments looking at heating and cooling, and insulation.

On special educational needs the Report is again very sensitive; it allows schools to exempt such students from sitting the tasks at the discretion of the headteacher but, on the other hand, it does allow the possibility of such students attempting the task and, if necessary, being provided with help and assistance (with the fact that such assistance has been given to be recorded). That proposal signals a way of assessment that is good for *all* students. Feuerstein has pioneered this approach primarily with children with special educational needs but the Russian psychologist Vygotski also looked at ways of assessing normal children that compared what they could do unaided with what they could do with the help of an adult or a peer – 'the zone of next development'.[7] The Report also recognises the dangers of gender and ethnic bias in assessment, but I think that we need to be more positive and to explore ways of investigating such bias much more vigorously. And finally, but no means least, the Report recognises the importance of teachers in the process of assessment. Mr Baker, himself, acknowledged that:

'The task ahead will not be done, nor done well, without

the initiative, effort and commitment of the education profession, in particular the teachers in the classroom.'[8]

The TGAT Report expands that notion and indicates the many ways in which teacher involvement is a condition for the success of the venture. Among their proposals are stress on the formative aims, a realistic timescale for phasing in the new system, adequate resources including in-service provision, and widespread consultation and discussion.

In this chapter, I examine four issues in particular. They are not by any means the only four that either cause me concern or are starting points for further development, but they do crystallise, for me, some of the possibilities within the TGAT Report. The four issues are:

1   The nature of attainment targets
2   Moderation
3   The publication and reporting of results
4   Implementation

1   *The Nature of Attainment Targets*
What are attainment targets, or benchmarks as Mr Baker sometimes calls them? We have had goals and we have had objectives for many years; attainment targets seem to be a new version of those. We also know from the experience of industry and commerce that clarifying goals both for the organisation and for the individual appears to be motivating and helpful.[9] But in education attainment targets are perhaps more difficult to formulate. To illustrate the nature of attainment targets I like to quote from Ted Wragg's column in *The Times Educational Supplement*. In the context of GCSE he illustrated grade criteria as follows. He felt, incidentally, that it was necessary to add three further grades to the bottom of the grading scale, those three grades to be reserved for Chelsea supporters. The criteria for those three grades were 'J' to put a thumb print on the paper, 'I' to put a neat thumb print on the paper, 'H' to colour the thumb print in Chelsea's colours. Then, rejoining the official grading scale, 'G' to spell history, 'F' to tell a history book from a maths book, 'E' to be able to put a history book under the shortest leg of a rickety table, 'D' to *understand* why they put a

history book under the rickety table, 'C' to be able to pass O level history, 'B' to know at least thirty useless dates and thirty meaningless facts and 'A' to recite the names of the whole of Wellington's army.

To prepare grade criteria for the GCSE, dozens of teachers were locked away in Newcombe House, the headquarters of the Secondary Examinations Council (SEC), to see if they could come up with improvements on Ted Wragg's proposals. I have looked through the accounts and annual reports of the SEC to try to work out how much the exercise cost, but unfortunately they do not analyse expenditure by individual projects. Nevertheless, I can confidently say that hundreds of thousands of pounds went in this venture to develop grade criteria. But that exercise has run into the sand in terms of producing *national* grade criteria. The current effort is devoted to something called performance matrices, that is, a presentation of criteria for assessing different grades that is derived from *particular* syllabuses, and from the work of candidates on examination papers and other forms of assessment on those syllabuses. Considerable work is scheduled for the development of performance matrices over the next three or four years. I think that it is too early to say whether performance matrices will be of any benefit – what they certainly will not do is to create a system of *national* attainment targets. Similar difficulties were experienced in Scotland where in their Standard Grade examination (which is, of course, a national examination operated by their only examination board) the grade criteria ran into severe problems. Within a matter of months of the new system being introduced, a committee had to be established to seek ways of simplifying the examination and the grade criteria. In particular, that committee recommended that grade criteria should *not* be used as devices for framing and organising assessment. They were excellent for clarifying goals and objectives for *teaching* but as *an assessment framework* it was felt that they were far too elaborate and complicated. One of the main problems in public examinations is undoubtedly the fact that there may be hundreds of different attainment targets but they still have to be aggregated and reported on a single scale for each subject. The multiplicity of targets is therefore the first problem. As Margaret Brown has pointed out, if you set up committees with the best of intentions, you can still find that attainment targets multiply like white mice.[10]

One of the high priests of the movement for the clear specification of educational objectives is the American, Jim Popham. In a recent article he has made it clear that too many goals (or too many attainment targets) can confuse people:

> 'Simply stated the most important lesson we have learned about the use of behaviourally stated objectives is that *less* is most definitely *more*. Too many objectives, because the decision makers will not attend to them, are completely dysfunctional.'[11]

The Mathematics Working Group has taken this lesson to heart, at least in theory. Its criteria for the development of attainment targets are that they should be broad based, accessible to all pupils, recognisable outputs of the educational process and in some cases taught in a cross-curricular context. They go on to say that 'our intention is that attainment targets should be relatively few in number'.[12] All the signs are that there will be more than a hundred for each age group. I would argue that we should look for *far fewer* than that: keep them few, keep them broad. In the Scottish Action Plan post 16, and a lot of work being done on modules and units here in London, the number of different defined targets is small: four or five – that is the sort of number that you would reasonably expect young people to keep in mind to frame their work. If you want only a few, you must have them broad. Overleaf I give an example of those being proposed in a context of science (Figure 5). I have deliberately chosen examples from the area of attitudes rather than more conventional and perhaps more easily devised objectives in the area of knowledge and understanding. They are interesting, but too specific in my view.

The TGAT Report proposes that one profile component (that is, one cluster of attainment targets) should be cross-curricular and therefore should reappear in other subject areas, but some modern approaches to the curriculum, for example in TVEI and pre-vocational courses, are much more fundamental

---

Attitudes

Attainment Target: Curiosity in relation to the activities undertaken, materials studied and used and issues discussed in the classroom.

The pupil:

- Shows interest in things which are new or familiar ones which are pointed out.

- Spontaneously questions new and familiar things even though interest may be shortlived.

- Seeks by questioning or action to find out about new and familiar things in the environment.

Figure 5

in the sort of cross-curricular skills they foster – both intellectual, such as the use of literacy and numeracy across the curriculum, and in the realm of social and personal skills – above all in cooperative learning rather than competitive learning. So I think that we must find ways of allowing those courses that provide interesting, helpful challenges to young people to survive within a national curriculum. I would suggest that it is in the way in which one formulates attainment targets that this is best achieved.

Attainment targets are based on the objectives model of education and there is substantial literature from the 1960s and 1970s – notably the work of Lawrence Stenhouse – which has much to say about the limitations of objectives.[13] I think that those limitations have been implicitly recognised by the Government when they indicate that there are not to be attainment targets in PE, art and music but just guidelines. We must avoid the mechanistic approach and the reductionism that the objectives model can easily lead to. In the words of Maurice Holt commenting on the national Consultation Document:

'The entire document is steeped in the mechanistic assumption that schools can be run like biscuit factories. Providing the skills and technology are there, backed by clear objectives and precise assessment, the right product will roll off the assembly line.'[14]

Objectives need to embody the spirit of education in the round. Some people might challenge me and say that juxtaposing education in the round with the very word 'objectives' is a mistake and a contradiction. Perhaps then we must look for broad aims (rather than objectives), aims stated in such a way that one can find ways of assessing them.

My next point about attainment targets concerns the degree to which they should be regarded as fixed. The whole of the national curriculum proposals are based on fixed, age-related targets. The model underlying national assessment is clearly that of graded assessment, but most graded assessment systems are not rigidly age-related but flexible. The idea is that you enter for the test or assessment *when you are ready.* This is certainly true in music and ballet. In graded assessment in mathematics in London (the GAIM Project), they too have broken away from age-related assessment. The student collects targets one by one and accumulates them for certification. There is no fixed route implied. Indeed the research of Margaret Brown and her colleagues, though indicating some common patterns, shows that pupils develop and learn in different ways.[15] More importantly, Rosalind Driver's work in science shows how many different ways and different routes there are to learning according to the concepts or, indeed, the misconceptions that young people bring with them to the classroom.[16] GAIM and other graded assessment projects have moved away from the notion that all fourth-year students take a test on a given day in June; rather, teachers monitor progress by the steady accumulation of targets. When the student has collected a defined group of targets then he or she can receive a certificate indicating the achievement of the corresponding level.

A second aspect to fixedness is the *pre-ordained nature* of attainment targets implied by the national curriculum. This is at variance with the powerful notion within records of achievement that students and teachers should negotiate, and set a limited number of future targets, in the light of the progress made and in the short term.[17] Perhaps that sort of negotiation of short-term targets will still be possible within a system that defines targets at only four stages separated by several years, but I nevertheless think that TGAT should encourage much more recognition of the value of pupil self-assessment and teacher/pupil review, that is, a discussion of whether targets have been reached as well as what targets are appropriate for the future. The model of assessment is not clearly defined within the TGAT Report. The use of terms like 'standard assessment task' rather than 'test' is still implying that assessment is done *to* the pupil rather than done *by* the pupil in cooperation with the teacher. I am suggesting, however, that there are ways, even within a system of fixed and age-related targets, to develop a more responsive system. In the longer term I suspect that the age-relatedness of the targets may disappear and that we may move to a system of graded assessment or assessment when ready. Such a system would still allow us to report that, by the age of 14, some 10 per cent of young people had reached level 5, 50 per cent had reached level 6 and so forth, so that a system of *reporting* at fixed ages does not necessarily mean a system of *testing* at fixed ages.

My final point about fixedness arises from the very nature of criterion-referencing. Current rhetoric has painted a picture of norm-referencing as bad and criterion-referencing as good. But in fact criterion-referencing reflects an impersonal abstract social need whereas norm-referencing recognises that 'the measure of mankind is man'. (Incidentally, I thought hard about how to make that last remark non-sexist but failed.) There is also a feeling that criterion-referencing and norm-referencing are the only two models available. In fact ipsative assessment, that is, assessment of the person against his or her own performance on a prior occasion – something which many many teachers do naturally in their assessment in the classroom – is a third powerful framework for assessment. The very notion of progress through levels implies an ipsative framework as much as it does a criterion-referenced one.

I have addressed at some length the issue of attainment targets, and their problems and possibilities, not least because there is still a massive amount of work to be done on attainment targets, not just by TGAT, but a task that will continue for many years to come as the curriculum working groups do their job. I think that there is much more scope for change and development in that field than the TGAT Report acknowledges.

2   *Moderation*

TGAT propose that results from national assessments (the standard assessment tasks) and the teachers' own assessments of individuals should be discussed in a process of group moderation, and any differences reconciled. In CSE, to some extent in GCE, and certainly in GCSE, the staff development role of group moderation has long been recognised, as well as its potency for promoting consultation and feedback to examining boards. Indeed, in one of the original CSE boards, the West Yorkshire and Lindsey Board, the model was of standards being determined locally by teacher groups and being fed *up* the system to the examining board, rather than imposed centrally and disseminated through the system of groups. The proposals for moderation within the TGAT Report are demanding professionally (but, as I have indicated, also rewarding professionally) and very time-consuming. I consider that the teachers' contract imposed by Mr Baker should be revised to reflect the amount of time that would be needed to do this part of the job adequately. I support the basic model of moderation; what I am unhappy about is the TGAT argument that, since the system will be time-consuming, there may have to be an acceptance that moderation in this group fashion does not take place for all profile components every year, and that, where there is no group moderation, test results should override the teacher assessment if there is any discrepancy.[18] That, in my view, is anti-teacher. I would suggest that there are other ways of using the test results, for example, with test results functioning as a moderating instrument as used by the Business and Technician Education Council (arising from work that my colleagues and I did at the beginning of 1980s), showing how a test coupled with other information can be used as a device to indicate where teacher-based assessment might be out of line with national standards.[19] That seems to me to be using tests to support and monitor teacher judgments rather than to supplant them.

3 The Publication and Reporting of Results

The TGAT Report distinguishes between those two words, proposing that the results of assessments should be *reported* to parents, to pupils and to others that have the right to know (though, of course, they also propose that an individual's results should be confidential to that individual and his or her parents). They then go on to recommend that the results should be *published* only in aggregated form and in context. It is interesting to note that the proposals for national assessment in Scotland have a much lighter touch – in other words, not only will the testing be just in literacy and numeracy rather than across the curriculum as a whole, but the results are to be given *only* to children and their parents; there is no proposal in Scotland that the results should be aggregated and published for each school and each classroom.[20] In England and Wales, though, the Government has every intention of publishing results for individual schools. On this matter the TGAT Report is in my view rather confused. It is the confusion between reporting and publication, and the naivety of the TGAT proposals, that I would like to comment upon especially. They recommend that national assessment results from a class as a whole and a school as a whole should be available to the parents of its pupils; they also recommend that there should be no requirement to *publish* aggregated results of the pupils at age 7. But then they say that these results should be made available to parents, governors and providers (presumably the LEAs and the DES). I believe that, with a system of nationally standardised assessment results, *reporting* to such groups will be equivalent to *publishing* the results, and publishing them classroom by classroom. Many parents will be tempted to provide that information to many other people, for example to prospective parents and to the local press. The TGAT proposals have, therefore, to be viewed as proposals for *publication* even at the age of 7.

My second worry concerns their proposal that the results for each school should be published without statistical adjustment, but in the context of a written account of socio-economic and other influences that are known to affect attainment. They argue that the publication of such results and the use of such results to compare schools' performance 'would be liable to lead to complacency if results were adjusted and to misinterpretation if they were not'.[21] And it is that quotation that provides the title for this chapter.

I cannot understand why they feel that adjusted results should lead to complacency. The ILEA received considerable publicity because of the figures published in answer to a Parliamentary Question in January 1988 that showed that the proportion of leavers from ILEA with five or more O level Grades A to C (or equivalent) put the Authority in 86th place out of 96 LEAs. Whereas we know, from all the research done by the DES and others such as Gray and Jesson, that once one takes into account background factors such as the level of deprivation in London (for example the number of one-parent families, and the number of children eligible for free school meals) ILEA examination results are very much in line with expectation.[22] That doesn't make the Authority complacent; nobody is saying that examination results in inner London are good enough. There are several important initiatives like the London Compact and the London Record of Achievement that provide a framework for all the work on assessment in secondary schools. These initiatives are designed to raise standards in the Authority's schools, and to give more young people the opportunity to achieve examination results and hence jobs. To suggest that our adjusted examination results make us complacent is a nonsense. I think that headteachers and governors are quite capable of looking at the actual results alongside the adjusted results school by school, and of seeking ways of improving them. I also think that complacency about adjusted examination results is no more likely than it is among schools who get good results just because they have favoured catchment areas. If I may quote again the same leader from *The Times* commenting on the unadjusted local authority league table; rather scathingly, it said:

'That Harrow's results are four times better than Barking's for an extra £70 a head reveals very little more than that middle class children tend to do rather better at school than working class children.'[23]

This supports TGAT's own argument that results with no adjustment are liable to be misinterpreted. I cannot understand why, having made that statement, they then go on to propose that no adjustment should be made. They are inviting the very misinterpretation to which they draw attention.

I concede that the ways that we have of adjusting school examination results are not perfect. Now is the time to do more research; indeed, I am working with Harvey Goldstein of the Institute of Education to improve our methods. Verbal comments explaining why pupils in particular schools do not get as good examination results as pupils in more favoured schools are likely to be ignored. With national assessment, we must therefore adjust results, as we do in the ILEA, to reflect the intake of each school.

4 Implementation

The TGAT Report is excellent in the way that it recognises the time, the preparation and the in-service work needed to implement such a complex and innovative system. They have learned lessons from GCSE INSET where phase 1 of the INSET had to be done *before* there were any syllabuses and specimen materials, which made the materials rather abstract and divorced from classroom practice. TGAT should note the work of Michael Fullan who shows, through his extensive research and development in Canada, the sorts of support systems that are needed for schools when major innovations are proposed.[24] In looking for a strategy to implement the London Record of Achievement and graded assessment in ILEA schools, we have drawn on Fullan's work and provided development officers who work in about four schools, spending a day each week in each school to help in a variety of ways – in in-service, in general classroom support, and in commenting on and helping to define goals; on the fifth day, they return to County Hall to share their experience with their fellow development officers. They provide support within the context and the ethos of the school, and they provide it on a regular basis that keeps people working to a timetable of development. I would suggest that one needs such assessment missionaries like the famous Cockcroft mathematics missionaries. I am not sure that TGAT has really taken delivery of the sorts of support and training that are going to be needed for what is, for many, a really new venture. Primary schools have no tradition of group moderation in the same way that secondary schools have, and must allow time and all sorts of trials to prepare them.

Also, to prepare for the implementation we need research and development. The Report seems to rest on the notion of item banking or task banking. Like the history of grade criteria, the history of item banking has many casualties along the way and we need to review those experiences. Extensive work is needed on test and task development, and I would highlight especially the need to develop ways of assessing bias within tests and indeed within teacher assessment, bias, that is, on the grounds of gender, race and social class.

Assessment is often seen as the culprit, the cause of many of our problems in schools. The 11+ is always held up as example of an assessment system that had (and still has in some areas) tremendous backwash not only on the curriculum of primary schools but on the attitudes and motivation of young people and their parents. But of course it wasn't the act of assessment that was the true problem, it was the act of selection, the fact that we decided that young people at the age of 11 should be sorted into sheep and goats. What is important is that we do not use national assessment as a new system for sorting and sifting as some fear it might be, particularly at age 11 when there are to be new kinds of institution like city technology colleges and grant-maintained schools. Nevertheless, I would urge that in the discussion of assessment we distinguish between the effects of assessment itself and the reasons why we have assessment.

Summary
I would like to end with a summary of my major points. In Chapter 1, Stuart Maclure called the Act 'allergic to systems',

particularly local education authorities, arguing that that is why there were proposals for opting out and for market choice. Within the context of national curriculum and national assessment, though, elaborate new systems are being created, systems that will make the bureaucracy of GCSE look small by comparison. The system will not be like that of TVEI, which was established under broad criteria that offered money for local creativity and local development; the system will not, therefore, allow teachers to 'take the money and run' as they have with a number of devolved developments like Technical and Vocational Education Initiative (TVEI) and Lower Achieving Pupils Programme (LAPP) in recent years. Nevertheless, within the national framework of the TGAT system, I believe that there is plenty of scope for improvement and autonomy. In particular, it is not too late to see pupils as active partners in the process of assessment and able to be assisted during assessment in the manner of Vygotski. It is not too late to limit the number of attainment targets, to widen their range and their scope, and to promote cooperative learning and assessment. It is not too late to move nearer a system of assessment at stages rather than ages (though the implications for the organisation of schools and classrooms still have to be thought about). It is not too late to look for publication of adjusted results; indeed, I am told that even if this is not recommended nationally it is still open to LEAs to publish adjusted results. Nor is it too late, of course, to do the research and development that would improve some of these proposals considerably – first, to look at the issue of bias and, second, to look at moderation using the national test as a post-hoc monitoring device rather than as an imposed device.

So I would urge those of you who face the same dilemma as I did to apply one of the criteria that I proposed in Figure 1, one that underpins the GCSE, that is, to look for *positive achievement*. I *can* make a positive assessment of the TGAT Report, particularly if I am allowed to re-negotiate some of Mr Baker's targets and to develop them further. There is some complacency in the Report; there is some misinterpretation; but by and large the proposals make assessment the servant of the curriculum rather than its dominating master.

Notes and References

1   National Curriculum: Task Group on Assessment and Testing, *A Report*, DES/Welsh Office, 1988.

2   *The Times*, 14 January 1988.

3   A Gallup Opinion poll in September 1987 (reported in the *Daily Telegraph*, 7 October 1987) showed that 71 per cent of parents supported written tests with 24 per cent against.

4   *National Assessment and Testing – A Research Response*, papers presented to the BERA Conference on 'Benchmark Testing', Kendal, British Educational Research Association, 1988.

5   National Curriculum: Task Group on Assessment and Testing Report, *A Digest for Schools*, DES/Welsh Office, 1988.

6   *Education*, 12 February 1988.

7   See, for example, *The Handbook of Human Intelligence*, ed. R. J. Sternberg, Cambridge University Press, 1982.

8   *The National Curriculum 5–16: A Consultation Document*, DES/Welsh Office, July 1987.

9   See, for example, *Appraisal and Target Setting* by D. Trethowan, Harper and Row, 1987.

10   See note 4.

11   'Two decades of educational objectives', James Popham, *International Journal of Educational Research*, Vol. 11, No. 1, 1987, pp. 31–41.

12   National Curriculum Mathematics Working Group, *Interim Report*, 1987, para. 4.4.

13   See, for example, L. Stenhouse, *An Introduction to Curriculum Research and Development*, Heinemann Educational, 1975.

14   Maurice Holt, 'Bureaucratic benefits', *The Times Educational Supplement*, 18 September 1987, p. 30.

15   B. Denvir; M. Brown and P. Eve *Attainment Targets and Assessment in the Primary Phase: Mathematics Feasibility Study*, DES, 1987.

16   The Children's Learning in Science Project at the University of Leeds.

17   The national evaluation of records of achievement supports the significance of pupil-teacher negotiation in improving classroom relationships and enhancing pupil motivation (P. M. Broadfoot, M. E. James, S. McMeeking, D. L. Nuttall and B. M. Stierer, *Records of Achievement: report of the national evaluation*, HMSO, 1988).

18   The use of statistical moderation in this manner would be permissible under the General Criteria of the GCSE National Criteria only in rare circumstances.

19   D. L. Nuttall and P. Armitage, *Moderating Instrument Research Project: a summary*, BTEC, 1985.

20   As reported in *The Independent*, 20 November 1987.

21   TGAT Report (see Note 1), para. 133.

22   DES Statistical Bulletins 16/83 and 13/84; J. Gray and D. Jesson, 'Exam results and local authority league tables', *Education and Training UK*, 1987.

23   See Note 2.

24   M. Fullan, *The Meaning of Educational Change,* New York, Teachers' College Press, 1982.

Postscript

At the time this paper was originally given as a lecture, the Task Group on Assessment and Testing was still at work, and some of the points made were designed to influence their deliberations. The three supplementary Reports of TGAT were published in June 1988.[1] The first supplementary Report reviews the reactions and comments that they had received in response to the original Report; it is defensive in tone, but clarifies one or two points, though making no significant changes. The second Report describes the consultations with subject associations. The third Report is the longest and the most significant. It elaborates the support structure needed for the system of national assessment and fleshes out the proposal for group moderation and INSET. In response to a Parliamentary Question on 7 June 1988, the Secretary of State for Education and Science accepted the basic framework of the TGAT proposals, including the notion of ten levels, and the need for teacher assessment. He felt, however, that the suggestions on the moderation system appeared 'complicated and costly'. He therefore asked the School Examinations and Assessment Council and the National Curriculum Council to review the issues with interested parties and, by implication, to propose a simpler and cheaper solution. He also agreed that there should be no legal requirement for schools to publish aggregated results for 7-year-olds, but strongly recommended that schools should do so.

No significant amendments were made to the Education Reform Bill before enactment in relation to national assessment. Many people, including myself, had not noticed, however, that Section 2 specified that the arrangements for assessing pupils should be 'at or near the end of each key stage'. This provision means that it would be difficult to have assessment on demand, in the fashion of graded assessment, and consequently more difficult to move towards a system of grouping pupils by stage rather than by age. In addition, this section makes it less likely that results of assessment at age 11 will be used in the process of selection for different kinds of school, since the results will be known only after most of the transfer decisions will have been made.

If the passing of the Act shed little further light on the detail of national assessment, the detailed proposals for the national curriculum in mathematics and science certainly did. The working groups reported in the summer of 1988, and the National Curriculum Council consulted widely over their proposals.[2] The Secretary of State made his views known as well, and the National Curriculum Council published a revised set of proposals for attainment targets and programmes of study.[3] The nature of attainment targets has thus begun to become clear. In mathematics, 14 attainment targets are proposed, closely resembling educational objectives in phraseology. For example, Attainment Target 2: Number is 'understand number and number notation', while Attainment Target 13: Handling Data is 'represent and interpret data'. Each target is then broken down into 10 levels (often illustrated with sample questions). For example, level 1 of Attainment Target 2: Number is 'count, read, write and order numbers to at least 10, and know that the size of a set is given by the last number in the count; understand the conservation of number' while level 9 has the description 'distinguish between rational and irrational numbers'. (The other part of the level 9 description that appeared in the original proposal, namely 'be able to express a positive integer as a product of primes' has disappeared from the National Curriculum Council's proposals.) Not all targets have 10 levels; indeed level 10 is not specified for Attainment Target 2. The 14 attainment targets are to be grouped, for reporting and assessment, into two profile components: the first comprises 'knowledge, skills, understanding and use of number, algebra and measures' while the second comprises 'knowledge, skills, understanding and use of shape and space and handling data'. Neither of these titles for the profile components seems designed for clear communication to parents and the public.

In science, 17 attainment targets are proposed. As in mathematics, each attainment target is differentiated, usually but not always with ten levels. For reporting and assessment, the attainment targets are to be grouped into two profile components. The first, consisting only of Attainment Target 1, covers 'exploration of science, communication and the application of knowledge and understanding'. The second, covering the remaining 16 attainment targets, comprises 'knowledge and understanding of science, communication, and the applications and implications of science'.

The working groups originally proposed rather more attainment targets (15 in mathematics and 22 in science) and more profile components (3 in mathematics and 4 in science). Some of the attainment targets were non-cognitive in nature reaching as far as 'personal qualities' in mathematics. The structure of attainment targets and profile components for each subject was generally welcomed during the consultation exercise, but the Secretary of State was not happy with these more affective targets. Flying in the face of majority opinion, but consistent with the preferences of the Secretary of State, the National Curriculum Council eliminated such targets and simplified the structure of profile components. There must consequently be some doubt as to the independence of the National Curriculum Council.

Finally, the reports of the working parties shed further light on the notion of Standard Assessment Tasks (SATs). Both reports indicate that they expect assessment to be carried out using naturalistic tasks arising from the normal work in the classroom, often occupying several hours of activity, exclusively at age 7 and substantially at other ages. The only example given of such a SAT appears in the mathematics report (para. 9.13): 'work in a group to plan, schedule and run a trip for your class'. This is considered suitable from age 11 upwards. No advice is given about the problem of assessing pupils in a group while at the same time assigning the achievement of each individual pupil to a specific level in each of a number of different attainment targets. The suggestions on assessment made so far confirm my opinion that a massive research and development exercise is required, and in many cases will have to solve as yet unsolved problems in educational measurement.

Notes to Postscript

1   National Curriculum: Task Group on Assessment and Testing, *Three Supplementary Reports*, DES/Welsh Office, 1988.

2   *National Curriculum: Mathematics for ages 5 to 16*, DES/Welsh Office, 1988. *National Curriculum: Science for ages 5 to 16*, DES/Welsh Office, 1988.

3   National Curriculum Council, *Mathematics in the National Curriculum*, York, National Curriculum Council, December 1988.

National Curriculum Council, *Science in the National Curriculum*, York, National Curriculum Council, December 1988.

4

Managerialism in Higher Education
Maurice Kogan

Higher education in Britain is under pressure to change its ways
of working to a degree unparalleled in any other country in the
world. The cuts in its funding have been drastic enough,
although equalled in some other countries. The most radical
changes have been in the relationship between institutions and
their state sponsors, and in the demands made upon them to
change their ways of working.

In this chapter I analyse the changing models of the
sponsorship of higher education which are the frame within
which concepts of management have been insinuated, and then
identify desirable and necessary components of management
before considering the extent to which these have been
converted into unreflecting managerialism.

In doing so, I will try hard to avoid two vulgar errors. The first
is to assume that there was ever a golden age of unalloyed
freedom in which the delights of collegiality reigned absolutely
supreme. I shall also try to avoid the silly assumption that
management does not matter, that it is avoidable, and that
higher education institutions were not due for an improvement
in the way in which they conducted their affairs.

Two Models of Higher Education Government
We have been brought up on a classic and autonomous model of
the government of higher education. It is an ideal model and one
which was never purely obtained in all universities let alone in
the whole range of British higher education institutions. But its
components are recognisable and, to my mind, remain strong.

The beau ideal has been that of the self-governing institution.

An essential prerequisite of self-governance was independence from financial pressure. Before the ending of the quinquennial grant system in the early 1970s, the universities were virtually free from financial pressure, and the polytechnics, too, were increasingly moving towards independence from local authorities whose grip was, in any case, weakened by the operation of the national pooling system. Either through the giving of grants by a benevolent state, or through private endowment, or both, the autonomous institution can set its own objectives and create its own programmes of research, scholarship, teaching and relationships with the outside world.

The autonomy was made legitimate because it seemed consistent with the nature of the higher education task. In its purest form, higher education was there to ensure that generation of knowledge which was essentially a pursuit for individuals, even when they worked in quite large teams. And the more individualistic, indeed the more deviant at a certain level, the more the academic could test received knowledge and create more and better of the same.

In this model, it is hardly appropriate to talk about the setting of objectives other than in terms of the inner psyche because the motive force is not that of pre-stated social consideration but of the disinterested and often serendipitous pursuit of the truth. It follows that the unit which makes decisions about what to do is not the state, even if it gives the money. It is not the institution, even if it protects and enables the academic to keep at work. Authority is not imposed by hierarchy working through managerial systems. It is that of Polanyi's Republic of Science, in which knowledge rules and subtle interactions contribute towards a science which is both coherent and pluralist. Exchanges are made and the values placed upon the exchanges are derived from the quality of the work. Authority derived from society is a weaker value.

The organisational format is, therefore, not managerial but collegial. Managerial hierarchies maximise collective force through stratifying power and authority according to assumed function and ability. By contrast, the collegium is a minimum organisation. The college comes together to admit new members, to establish minimum standards, usually through its admission rules, and to divvy up the common resources. The strongest academic systems in the world and, indeed in this country, do not require shared objectives or common working patterns. They act collectively when they have to and compensate, perhaps, for their displays of autonomy by eating together and joining together in occasional rituals.

In Britain, until very recently, important components of this model held true, but on a steep sliding scale according to the status of the institution. It held true because it was assumed that the interests of society and of the academy coincided. The academy was trusted to educate and train a functioning elite and to deliver the knowledge that would sustain the economy and the society. It, too, could read the papers, and read off social needs as well as people in Whitehall or in industry.

There was, therefore, what some would call a socio-technological defence of these arrangements. Social or organisational arrangements were predicated upon assumptions about the nature of the task to be performed. And it is heartening to see how well it was performed. I do not read here from an AUT bulletin but from no other than the Jarratt Report:

> 'The UK universities make outstanding contributions to our national life. Their . . . degree courses are shorter than those of any other developed country and their wastage rate is low not least because of their emphasis on small group teaching and personal tuition. They play the leading role in maintaining and advancing scholarship in the humanities and the social sciences, where their achievements are high by international standards. They carry out the greater part of the pure research in the United Kingdom and much of the applied research in which the future scientific and technological development depends . . . They underpin in culture and the arts the quality of national life.'

Similar statements can be found in most of the other documents to which I have referred. One has to ask why, if these statements are true, entirely different systems have suddenly become necessary?

The opposite model is that to which government policy is now leading us. It is that of the dependent institution. It is one in which the objectives are not set by the inhabitants but by the sponsors. The academics will still determine how to do it, but ultimately what should be done, and why, will be determined by external social forces. This is, of course, no new thing in the long perspective of the history of higher education. In the past, the Church, the state, the world of employment, have all had control over bits of higher education. Our teacher training institutions have, of course, always been tied quite closely to patterns of demand and supply established by the state. Their development into broader functions has again been closely circumscribed by the national sponsors. Leave aside the assumptions about the objectives of polytechnics as stated in the White Paper of 1966 and Anthony Crosland's Woolwich speech (1965), we ought to recall how the civic universities when first established in the nineteenth century were expected to pursue quite particular functions related to industrial growth. In the end, however, what some call academic drift and what I call academic maturity ensured that they, of course, became real higher education institutions and not simply appendages to the economy.

In other countries dependency has been far stronger than here. But how fascinating to observe that just as we, whilst being praised to the skies by Jarratt and others, are being pulled into a dependency model. Many of the systems in continental Europe, take the Finns and the West German universities as examples, are simultaneously being pushed onto the open market for their resources at the same time as they are being given greater freedom from prescription so that they can become more self-accountable.

The dependency model is not based upon trivial value assumptions. It assumes that higher education is no different from any other public service; it is there to meet national needs in terms of the manpower required for the economy and to produce knowledge useful to the society.

These two ideal models have never lived in isolation from each other. Most institutions operate on mixes of them. They have been largely dependent on the state, within generous assumptions of autonomy, but have increasingly found it necessary to take on work whose objectives are determined, at

minimum, in consultation with outside forces. A whole spate of
Master's courses emerged, responding to external demands and
not simply pursuing the academically elegant and exquisite. And
contract research grew massively in the 1960s and 1970s. The
difference between then and what might become now, is that
academics accepted or rejected these developments on their
own criteria. They did not have to do what they were told in
order to keep in employment. Their substance was not
determined by a string of ad hoc contracts.

Let me complete this first descriptive part of my chapter by
linking the two models with the concepts of management and
managerialism. There has never been difficulty about the
concept of a system of higher education in which social and
economic purposes are expressed by sponsoring departments.
The Robbins expansion was allowed on the assumption that it
was possible simultaneously to satisfy student demand and the
needs of the economy, an expansion not universally welcomed
by Vice-Chancellors. There was no explicit statement of
national objectives. Those objectives that could be read off from
the agreements to pay grants were left to the institutions to
interpret in their own ways. Such a system might be rightly
criticised as being somewhat weak in its management
propensities. For one thing, it did not produce a large enough
higher education system, partly because it was not geared well
enough to developments in the upper forms of the schools. But
at least it did not suffer from the artificial elements of the
managerialism which is now developing.

Components of Management
Before embarking on that, let me try to outline components of
management which concern resources, rule setting and
development. Any organisation, no matter how committed to the
individual freedoms of its members, has to secure its resources,
distribute them effectively, pay attention to the outcomes and
evaluate performance. Even the richest American universities
devote an incredible amount of skill to sustaining and extending
their resources. In the UK, securing adequate resources is
certainly a management task of a high order. Dealing with the
DES, the University Grants Committee (UGC), the National

Advisory Body for Public Sector HE (NAB) or their successor bodies has always been and will always be a task demanding great ability, in reconciling conflicting demands within the institution and presenting them persuasively to the sponsors. It entails, or course, judgments on the value of what is being offered as against at least some general vision of what the institution is for. Call that setting objectives and then determine the financial allocations related to those objectives if you like.

But if managers must thus define, reconcile and persuade, that management of itself does not generate resources. It is academic groups who persuade the UGC of the quality of their research, or the NAB of the quality of courses, or other sponsors of their ability to give value for money. And it remains an open question whether it is administrators who are necessarily the best qualified to decide how to use the institution's resources rather than the academics who create them. A directorate plainly must analyse what is coming in and where it is going but the determination of choice is, in my submission, still something to be negotiated between administration and the academic producers. This is, of course, largely what happens now. But the Jarratt expression turns its back on such negotiation by creating strong institutional planning instruments, good in themselves, but which avoid any attempt to create interactive modes.

There will indeed be critical points at which institutional leadership and its administration must act strongly. At times of great reductions, administrators – I am avoiding the use of the word manager because that pre-empts my point – will have to decide, what academics can never decide without great noise and steam, such issues as which department might close. Administrators, too, might be more objective than the academics in pressing the case for new markets or in identifying serious weaknesses which the academic might not eradicate for themselves. The whole area of resources, then, needs strong and clear administration. It does not, however, dispose of the question of who will ultimately decide.

A second function concerns the administration of collective rules for academic behaviour. Academics determine criteria for student admission and for assessment. But administration has to make sure that the rules are consistent across the institution, that contracts are made properly and kept faithfully. Such rules cannot be individualistic but, by definition, are collective. They thus embody control and coherence but are, again, meaningless unless they ultimately refer to behaviour consistent with academic development.

A further set of tasks arise from the second and the first. It concerns institutional development. We academics cannot have it all ways. Individualist academics are rarely concerned with the development of the portfolio of the whole institution. Certainly a Vice-Chancellor or Director, coming from the academic world themselves, but now required to take a holistic view of the future, will be in the institutional development game. I will later argue that powerful departments are a feature of the good institution. But the stronger the departments, the stronger the reciprocal need for high quality administration that can set the development created by departments within the wider setting of resources, fairness between competing constitutents of the institution and concern for those interests which the institution is not yet meeting.

Financial and rule setting work, and planning in a developmental sense are, then, key elements of the management task. They require high technical ability, political skill and consume vast amounts of time. They constitute key managerial tasks for administrators but, as I have indicated, there are elements of them in which the academics have a place. We need courageous institutional leaders and technically able administrators. Administration and planning systems need to be stronger. But that does not entail the kind of administrative triumphalism which the official reports, and their accountants turned into management consultant advisers, would create. There are now institutions which accommodate institutional planning which looks to new markets and attempts to develop a mission, but which also take care to incorporate the working units' aspirations in their plans. Some look as if they might not care too much for the latter.

Managerialism
If management is an essential prerequisite to the successful achievement of higher education's purposes, it yet remains a

second order characteristic. The feature of the official literature to which I object is that it seems to have become a self-sufficient and self-justifying objective in its own right, taking on imperatives of its own as if they can be separately endorsed from higher education's primary objectives.

Much of my criticism must be based upon statements of intention rather than actual movements in the institutions. To a large extent the changes have not had time to work their way through the system. As yet, we are not blessed with the two new Funding Councils. Those curious brands of applied utilitarianism, performance indicators, have yet to be fully installed. The stimulus of working on contract is not yet available to us. So our primary evidence are the words written down in a series of major reports.

Those reports are the 1985 Jarratt Report on efficiency in universities, NAB's *Management for a Purpose*, the Croham Report on the University Grants Committee, the 1987 White Paper, the documents, reproduced in such a way that their authors seemed ashamed of them, on the contracting arrangements. More recently, there are the highly contested provisions of the Education Reform Act which give the Secretary of State those extraordinary powers which he now says will be used so sparingly and for such residual purposes that one wonders why he wants to take them anyway. Between them, these statements give us a pretty good idea of the trend in government thinking. They also show the extent to which leading academics in positions of power and status seem willing to play along with them.

Managerialism in higher education is based on the assumption that the institution and the system to which it becomes subordinate can specify objectives within which those of the basic units can be subsumed. It further assumes that the ability to determine and control the pursuit of objectives can be distributed hierarchically. Its moral justification is that higher education outcomes should or ought to be determined and judged outside itself and in terms of social rather than intellectual criteria. It is noticeable that this creed has been spelt out in most detail for the universities. They have been treated like religious houses in the early sixteenth century, full of libidinous abbots and corrupt nuns and most in need of reform. Our Sir Thomas Cromwell is Sir Alex Jarratt, formerly a second tier civil servant and now responsible for the fortunes of Reed International. He comes to the higher education scene, however, not only by virtue of those essential prerequisites of managerial wisdom but because he is the Chairman of the Council of the University of Birmingham.

The Jarratt Report is the most important of all the documents, not only because it is so explicit in its managerialism, but because it recruited the support of distinguished academics, including five present or former Vice-Chancellors or their equivalents, as well as the Chairman of the UGC and a university registrar.

Let us take some of the Jarratt prescriptions in more detail. First, they noted that university objectives and aims were defined only in very broad terms. We could immediately challenge the assumption that that is a bad thing. If we have it right, a university or any other higher education institution is essentially concerned with the development of specialist knowledge at the expert level. It addresses problems covering virtually the whole universe of human experience. What kind of objectives can entail all of these? Organisational objectives which do not take account of the expected outcomes are likely to be vacuous. But the nature of our outcomes is closely linked to the modes of production. Knowledge creation is, as I have already suggested, primarily individualistic or even idiosyncratic rather than collective in its nature. Name one Nobel Prize winner who worked within objectives set by his institution, let alone the system.

So the objectives game needs to be tied down quite closely if it is not simply to be vacuous. Certainly one would expect institutions to enter into long-term planning in as much as they must relate their resources to some reasonable prediction of likely demand. That is not at issue. The issue is rather whether statements of ultimate purpose are to be based on generalised prescriptions which must then be disaggregated, or whether the institution does not see itself as capable of incorporating multiple states of knowledge generation and dissemination within the broadest indicative frame of social objectives. Are the objectives to be derived from the nature of knowledge or imposed by the economy and government? In some societies, objectives of the latter kind might be necessary. A new country with no tradition of higher education may need, or may not be able to afford, higher education which does more than train its elites and provide rudimentary applied research for the economy. But I thought we were now a developed country.

Other aspects of Jarratt one need not challenge. The discussion of academic strengths and weaknesses is certainly a task for academic management and Jarratt rightly pointed out that it rarely happened. Staff evaluation could be improved. Better information systems have certainly been needed.

Let me now move onto another Jarratt point which concerns structures. They wrote that the reasons why planning and resource allocation had not been sufficiently dynamic were that:

> 'There are strong forces within each university. These include large and powerful academic departments together with individual academics who sometimes see their academic discipline as more important than the long-term well-being of the university which houses them. We suggest that in our view universities are first and foremost corporate enterprises to which subsidiary units and individual academics are responsible and accountable. Failure to recognise this will weaken the institution and undermine its long-term vitality.'

A more inaccurate statement of what constitutes a good higher education institution cannot be imagined. The well-being of the institution is important only because it ensures the good work of the individuals who work in it. Any academic enterprise which does not have powerful academic departments and powerful individual academics who cherish their academic discipline above all else, will be second rate or worse. What is the nature of the task being performed here? Who can define it if not the academics themselves? The institution may well be more than a holding company because it alone can maintain the boundary between academic work and the community which sponsors it. But the essentials of academic work must surely reign supreme above those of institutional policy making.

Moreover, they are not even consistent. They maintain that there is an essential and logical link between establishing a corporate enterprise and translating the Vice-Chancellor from the role of the leading scholar and *primus inter pares* – admittedly an idealised picture of the traditional Vice-Chancellor – into what they describe as 'the style of Chief Executive, bearing the responsibility for leadership and effective management of the institution'. Now the Sizer research and writings by such as Martin Trow have rightly emphasised the importance of leadership in higher education. But leaders can operate with collegia or with hierarchy. Both need leadership. Just observe how the Jarratt Report deplores strong leadership and power at the working levels of the institution, namely, the departments, but wants it far stronger in the Chief Executive style Vice-Chancellor. So we don't mind individual power as long as it is well away from the working level. One is bound to ask whether the Master of St John's College, Cambridge really believed in this kind of model which was written in the report that he signed.

And so the analysis goes on down the line. They identify, for example, the head of department as a key managerial role. He or she must possess the requisite managerial capabilities. His duties, responsibilities and reporting lines should be made clear. He must also consult and inform his colleagues. In other literature in the field a member of Jarratt, Geoffrey Lockwood and his colleague John Davis, convert Deans into something they call middle managers.

But if Jarratt takes its analysis, if that be the word, down, if that be the the the word, to the level of the head of department, there is no analysis whatsoever of the primary production level, namely, the individual teacher and researcher. We get no picture of what they are supposed to do except that they have got to be accountable and that they have got to fulfil the institution's objectives. I do not know of any competent organisation analysis which does not specify the tasks to be performed so that the social and organisational relationships can then be developed around them.

All of this makes the document a thoroughly incompetent piece of work. Better is *Management for a Purpose* produced by the NAB Good Management Practice Group. It maintains that 'people work best if they are not only committed to what they are doing but also have control over the resources and activities involved'. Better. But even so, it uses language which does not tee up with what I would regard as conditions for good academic work. It refers, for example, to characteristics that are to be found in any well-run institution. Staff are 'to understand clearly what they are required to do and their accountability for it'.

The Croham Report of 1987 was in many respects the best of the documents. It was not Croham's fault that the Government mistook or deliberately distorted the proposals for a contractual relationship between the public and the universities. They were obviously thinking in terms of a kind of social contract to be expressed through each university's academic plan. Some joker within the DES must have converted that notion to the idea of breaking up the academic task into contractual fragments. Nor is it their fault that the concept of deficiency grant has been converted into the notion of contractual funding. But on the constitutional arrangements, too, they are in line with Jarratt in that they believed that higher education should be a part of the economic machine. The Chairman of the Universities Funding Council should be an eminent figure with substantial experience outside the academic world. Up to now he has always been a distinguished academic. The words 'industry and commerce' are those used to denote the origins of the non-academic members, with this change in direction, albeit mitigated by the academic identity of the Director-General, the notion of the collegium running its affairs within broad policy frameworks set by the Government goes out of the window.

That may be a legitimate choice for government to make. I just wonder whether this Government would accept that when they eventually leave office and Mr Livingstone comes into power, it will not be a captain of industry but, perhaps, Linda Bellos who becomes Chairperson of the Funding Council. My point is not entirely facetious. If social criteria rather than those of the academy are to rule, are there any limits to the social criteria that might be allowed to rule?

It is obvious, then, that control over the academic enterprise is to be moved from that of its traditional centre, the individual academic, working within a basic unit, to the whole system. It assumes that there can be collective objectives for higher education beyond those of the general Robbins Report kind. It assumes that objectives can be set with such precision that evaluative frames can follow them in the form of lists of weighted performance indicators. The Committee of Vice-Chancellors and Principals (CVCP) and the Committee of Directors of Polytechnics wisely note that performance indicators should be used informationally rather than as stringent frames for allocating resources. But given the surrounding managerialist rhetoric there is a danger that they will be used as manipulable categories by those who do not master the individualised nature of higher education work.

I must express doubt about the necessity for all of this systems building. The government of the day can assert whatever higher education policy it likes, be it a shift to science and technology and business studies, or an increase or decrease in the APR, or changes in balances between the genders recruited for higher education. It has the power to make at least broad shifts in the range of institutional activity a condition upon which grant will be given. Does it then really have to compel the institutions to chant obediently the managerialist rhetoric? Can it be so sure that the most productive academics are those who state their objectives, convert their Vice-Chancellors or Directors into Chief Executives, call the Deans middle managers and the heads of departments first line managers?

Conclusion
Let me finish by making two further points of elaboration. A few of us from Brunel University have recently been studying the way in which nine very varied institutions of higher education have responded to external influences. We found that individual academics in those forty-nine departments were well aware of the pressures being placed upon them and their institutions. Changes in the curriculum, varying greatly across the subject range and greatly in their intensity, are taking place because of teachers' own concerns for the employment prospects of their students. The teaching agenda is modified in

some universities because research is also modified by the changing pattern of grants which are available. In some institutions there is what we call coerced change – when a whole department is closed or whole disciplinary structure replaced by thematised courses designed to meet employment needs. But for the most part change occurs not only because management wishes it to be so but because teachers themselves are capable of making their own calculations. They know there is a balance to be struck if they are to survive both in terms of their own academic values and in terms of what the market will pay for.

Now it may be that those processes could be enhanced by the chanting of managerial mantras. Given severe changes in resources there can be no doubt that institutions need to have an academic plan. But need the process of forming that academic plan be more than the negotiative bargaining procedures brought into a rational and quantified format?

So much of this is that it is an unnecessary and derogatory process being applied to a system which ranks very high among the higher education systems of the world. One has a kind of a moral objection as well as a logical one to the managerialist trend. A distinguished member of this institution puts it well. Guy Neave writes that:

> 'Institutional leadership cannot construe its tasks simply in terms of efficiency, cost saving and greater accountability alone. It has also to be concerned with restating the vision of the university as a value allocating body in our society . . . Leadership can be reduced to an analysis of functions, tasks, procedures, techniques, manipulations and the resources to do this. They are a necessary part. But without an informed – and shared – vision they are little more than redoubling the means whilst the ends stand forgotten.'

In my own case, and speaking as somebody who worked as a central government administrator for fourteen years before becoming an academic, I can only note the discrepancy between what seems to preoccupy those who have produced these reports and what motivates our daily work. Those who write these reports have not attended to the real tasks of higher education or to the working environments which they require. And one sometimes wonders whether the institutions which Kenneth Baker, Sir Alex Jarratt, Lord Croham and the DES planners seem eager to create are the kind of institution that they would like their own children to have attended.

References

Croham Report (1987) *Review of the UGC.* London: HMSO.
DES (1987) White Paper *Higher Education: Meeting the Challenge.* London: HMSO.
Jarratt Report (1985) Report of the Steering Committee for Efficiency Studies in Universities. (CVCP).
National Advisory Body for Public Sector Higher Education (1987) *Management for a Purpose.* A Report of the Good Management Practice Group. London: BSC Print Ltd.
Sizer, J. (1982) 'Performance Indicators for Institutions of HE' in McCormick, R. (ed.) *Calling Education to Account.* London: HEB.

5

The Abolition of the ILEA

Tessa Blackstone

Introduction

I have lived in inner London for the last twenty-five years –
nineteen of them in Stoke Newington. My children were
educated in inner London primary and secondary schools. My
first job after graduation was part-time teaching in what became
an inner London polytechnic. I have been a parent governor in
an ILEA primary school and was for many years a governor of a
county secondary school and a voluntary-aided secondary
school in the ILEA. Late in 1982 I was appointed Deputy
Education Officer (Resources) and on the abolition of the GLC
in 1986 became Clerk to the Authority and Director of
Education. I have therefore seen the Authority from a variety of
perspectives: parent, governor, chief officer, and last, but not
least, as a Professor at the Institute of Education.

I am not sure whether all this makes me well qualified to
speak about the ILEA or disqualifies me to do so. But I want to
emphasise that I wish to be as dispassionate and objective as
possible. No organisation is without its faults – and that
includes the ILEA. I have no intention of dwelling entirely on its
strengths. I want also to say something about its weaknesses.
However, I must make clear from the start that I am strongly in
favour of the maintenance of a unitary education authority in
inner London and passionately opposed to dismembering the
existing authority and giving the borough education powers. I do
not believe this is in the interest of children, young people or
adults in the capital. I need to make this clear at the outset
because I have been quoted out of context by the Secretary of
State in the House of Commons and by the Parliamentary

Under-Secretary in the House of Lords.

Education in inner London has been provided by a single authority for over one hundred years. Many of the London schools used today were built by the London School Board established in 1870. The London School Board was succeeded in 1902 by the Education Committee of the London County Council, many of the hallmarks of which can still be found in today's ILEA. Much of the educational provision in inner London bears little relationship to the boundaries of London boroughs created nearly a century later in 1964. A common feature of school and, more so, college provision is of some institutions on the boundaries of a borough recruiting equally from an adjacent borough; one further education college has sites in three different London boroughs. This integrated provision serving inner London has now been abolished.

Inner London's Needs

The area served by the Inner London Education Authority includes seven of the ten most deprived local authority areas in Britain. In 1980, H M Inspectorate commented:

> 'The ILEA is faced with problems of a type, range and complexity unmatched in other local education authorities and any assessment of its performance should take account of the circumstances in which it operates.'

On most – if not all – measures of need, the difficulties faced by inner Londoners and the needs to be met by their education service have been steadily increasing since 1980. Average figures mask *wide variations* across inner London, between areas of considerable wealth and affluence and acute poverty and disadvantage.

Of those children whose parental occupation is known, 28 per cent of primary children and 20 per cent of secondary pupils now have unemployed parents (up from 19.9 per cent and 15.8 per cent respectively in 1983). Twenty-seven per cent of primary children and 28 per cent of secondary pupils come from one-parent families – twice the national average. The 1985 figures were 25 per cent and 26 per cent respectively. Nearly half of all ILEA pupils now qualify for free school meals – 49 per cent in primary schools and 45 per cent in secondary schools. In 1983, just 37 per cent (primary) and 33 per cent (secondary) qualified.

The 1987 ILEA language census found that a total of 172 different languages are spoken in ILEA schools. Nearly one pupil in four (22.7 per cent) speaks a language other than English at home. The equivalent figures for previous years were 14 per cent (1981), 16 per cent (1983) and 19 per cent (1985). While for many pupils, bilingualism is an opportunity and an advantage, the number of children who need help with English is increasing in inner London. In 1985, there were 35 589 such pupils. By 1987, the number had grown to 44 448.

Inner London is the most densely populated conurbation in the country – 26 times greater than the country as a whole. Inner London's population density is one and a half times that of Liverpool – the next most densely populated city – and twice that of Birmingham and Manchester. Half of ILEA's secondary schools and a quarter of primary schools use buildings put up in the last century – a much higher proportion than anywhere else. Because of their age, these buildings cost more to maintain, while land and building costs in inner London are at least a third higher than elsewhere in the country.

Strengths of the ILEA

The ILEA has three major strengths:

- the resources to plan and provide good city wide services;
- the confidence and scope to innovate;
- a strong moral purpose.

Central resourcing is provided over an area of 114 square miles to serve a child population of nearly 300 000 pupils, a student population of over 200 000 and an adult population of a quarter of a million. The scale and expertise of that resourcing is unequalled elsewhere. The Inspectorate is a good example. It is able to do two things: attract high quality staff (because of the career prospects and scope of activity) and inspect and advise across all phases of education and the whole of the curriculum. Whereas the outer London boroughs have between ten and twenty inspectors, the ILEA has 171.

All ILEA schools, wherever they are, receive four types of inspectorate advice and support:

1   Locally-based inspectors who are specialists in primary, secondary or special education. Their role is to advise headteachers in their division about overall policies in their schools. They have extensive experience as headteachers or deputy heads. Although based at divisional offices, they are members of an authority-wide team drawing expertise and support from colleagues elsewhere.

2   Specialist inspectors covering every subject in the school curriculum. These inspectors are recruited for their special expertise in a subject area and many of them have national reputations in their own field. They work across the whole authority and so are able to compare standards and spread good practice throughout inner London. In addition to specialist inspectors in English, mathematics and other mainstream subjects ILEA has specialist inspectors in drama, craft, design technology, health education – and classics.

3   Areas not covered by the traditional school curriculum also have inspectorate support. These include English as a second language, the teaching of 'heritage' languages, computer studies, health education and the special educational needs of pupils. No other authority can match the network of inspectors and advisory teachers helping teachers in these challenging areas.

4   The ILEA also has specialists in the educational needs of children suffering every kind of major disability – many of them national experts in their field.

In small borough authorities, the advisory and inspectorate service often numbers less than ten. With such small teams, individuals inevitably have to share a wide range of responsibilities. A general inspector may have to cover different phases (for example, primary and secondary) as well as taking responsibility for one or more subject areas. The science adviser is likely to have to cover all the sciences and probably computer studies as well. A humanities adviser would be responsible for history, geography, economics, social studies and religious education. Some curriculum areas may not be covered at all.

Another example is the careers service which provides careers guidance on employment or further and higher education to young people throughout inner London. A young person in Deptford, for example, can visit the local careers office, have advice from a careers officer and, through the computerised jobs register be informed of countless available jobs across the metropolis. Conversely, an employer by making a single telephone call can have access to a register covering people looking for jobs from Spitalfields in East London to Southfields in South West London.

Similarly, the Education Welfare Service, stretching across inner London, not only allows work to be coordinated and strategic planning to take place but also can afford specialist education welfare officers to work with homeless families or with the children of travellers who are constantly on the move and whose education is seriously disrupted. Research in the ILEA has always been one of the Authority's strengths with its Research and Statistics branch having national status. The research which it has carried out has provided information about needs, about strategies for effecting changes or improving practice. It has been used not just by the ILEA but other LEAs –and even the DES in planning change.

Resources and the confidence to innovate have been a hallmark of the ILEA. Some of the ideas have created white elephants – like its education television service; many have provided the springboard for developments to improve the quality of education.

In a mixture of openness and perhaps rashness the Authority invited David Hargreaves, then Reader in Education at Oxford University, to lead a committee of enquiry into secondary education 'with special reference to pupils under achieving'. When that was complete it had the courage to publish the findings and, following consultation, proceed to implement the changes recommended in *Improving Secondary Schools.*
Following the Hargreaves Report came the Thomas review on *Improving Primary Schools* and finally *Educational Opportunities for All?* on meeting special education needs.

About to come to fruition in 1990, when the first new inner London LEAs may come into existence, is the London Record of Achievement. In that year all 16-year-old school leavers will be provided with a full record of their achievement in all areas of the curriculum. Earlier in 1987 the Prince of Wales launched 'Compact' a scheme of cooperation between achools and employers in the East End to ensure jobs for school leavers in return for agreed levels of attendance, punctuality and basic skills. Not only was that innovative, it hardly matches the stereotype of a lunatic left education authority. The failure to give the ILEA credit for introducing 'Compact' was notable when the Government announced it would ask for bids for the new 'Compacts' around the country.

A strength, and an irritation to its critics, has been the strong moral purpose of the Authority. Rooted in the Fabian ideals of the London County Council, the ILEA continued the tradition of benevolent welfarism. In the 1980s this was replaced by a sharper egalitarian thrust with emphasis on anti-racist and anti-sexist initiatives. However, whatever criticisms are made of the Authority it has not been charged with corrupt or illegal practices. Its moral or political purpose may be anathema to its opponents but, unlike local government in the North East in the 1960s or Merseyside in the early 1980s, London education has *never* been synonymous with sharp practice.

Moreover, the Authority's strong sense of moral purpose has been reflected in its commitment to educational policies which either *extend* provision to a much higher proportion of the population than is common in other authorities, or *invest much more* in certain kinds of *existing* provision to ensure that disadvantaged groups have a better deal than is common elsewhere. I will give two examples in each category: nursery education and adult education first; special education and provision to meet the needs of black and ethnic minority children second.

Nursery Education

For some years the Authority has aimed to provide a nursery place for every 3- or 4-year-old whose parents want one. In 1987–88 nearly 24 000 pre-school age children received nursery education in inner London – about 40 per cent of all 3- and 4-year-olds. In 1987 the ILEA had forty-nine nursery schools and 508 nursery classes attached to primary schools (with another thirty-one about to open in the pipeline). The ILEA spent £30.5 million on nursery education in 1987–88.

Its plans for expansion of nursery education have been guided by the recommendations of an ILEA working party. Among its recommendations were: nursery education should be expanded as quickly as possible; plans for new nursery schemes should give high priority to social and economic need; more full-time places should be provided; there should be better coordination of planning and information to parents. The Authority's policy is to have a nursery class for every primary reception class. There is a shortfall – mainly in the voluntary school sector. This is because the DES building allocations for voluntary schools are very low. Expansion of nursery education is also greatly handicapped by the national shortage of nursery teachers and nursery nurses.

Adult Education

Inner Londoners have more adult education opportunities than anyone else in the country. Some 270 000 students sign up for courses each year – that is, one Londoner in seven over the age of 16. Although only 5 per cent of the population of England and Wales live in inner London, 15 per cent of all the adult education is provided by ILEA.

The eighteen adult education institutes place a special emphasis on work with the unemployed and those facing other forms of hardship and disadvantage. About two-thirds of all adult students pay reduced or no fees because they are retired, unemployed, on low incomes or attending basic education classes. A recent survey of adult students showed that more than 40 per cent of adult students had no previous qualification. One in four gave the major reason for enrolling as the chance to make up for a lack of previous educational opportunities. Almost half of all adult students are black or from other ethnic minorities.

Adult education institutes are informal places where students are made to feel comfortable and confident about discussing their learning needs. Using the flexibility allowed to institutes to decide on how they use their resources, they cooperate with local groups and agencies to provide courses at short notice, as the need arises. This is in addition to the full programme of courses publicised in each institute's annual prospectus. Institutes also cooperate closely with other sectors. Courses for parents, family workshops and home visits to parents with pre-school children are organised in cooperation with schools. 'Open college' networks – increasing access to further and higher education – are increasingly organised in cooperation with colleges and polytechnics. With a governing body on which the local community is heavily represented, each adult institute makes most of its own decisions on resources, curriculum and management, within broad guidelines laid down by the ILEA. The ILEA also supports an education advice service in each borough for adults who need help choosing the right course.

Special Education
About 8300 children in inner London have a 'statement' of special educational need – that is, their needs are so severe as to require a statement. For more than 97 per cent of these children, their needs are met in the ILEA's own schools, colleges and special units. The ILEA provides a more comprehensive range of special educational services than any other local education authority. Of the children with statements, 6600 are in special schools, 495 are in specialist units in mainstream schools and 1200 receive individual support in mainstream schools. Further education colleges provide both specialist courses and support for mainstream courses. For children without statements, there is a range of linked and unified support services.

Support services for those with special needs are far better than elsewhere. They include peripatetic support teams, long and short stay off-site centres and truancy units, and a central advisory team; child guidance services (sixteen consultation and advice centres for pupils, parents and schools); four courses at FE colleges: eleven specialist units for language-impaired children (ten attached to mainstream schools, one to a MLD school). In addition, there are: a team of special education inspectors with a specialist in every area of disability or learning difficulty; the Educational Computing Centre, coordinating development of software for special education; a special education resources team; a teachers' centre for special education; an individual tuition service with a centre in each division for children who are temporarily unable to go to school; fifteen specialist officers; a senior youth officer responsible for specialist youth work; three social work services – psychiatric, school and education; eighty-two educational psychologists including specialists in different disabilities and learning difficulties; and finally, a wide range of special courses in adult education institutes.

Multi-ethnic Provision

One in four of inner London's pupils speak or use a language other than English. In colleges and adult institutes, the proportion is higher. For many of these young people, bilingualism is a positive advantage. But nearly 45 000 pupils in inner London schools need help with English. The level of language support given by the ILEA and the coordination of London-wide services to ensure equal access to educational opportunities is therefore vital.

At present the Authority provides support on a generous scale. Six inspectors and 190 teachers – deployed across the Authority in thirty-five teams – give both central and local support. The top priorities for the team are:

1   Direct language teaching support for bilingual pupils. Without fluency in English, pupils' educational progress is held back. The teachers work mainly in primary schools, which, unlike secondary schools, do not usually have specialist teachers of ESL on the staff.
2   In-service training for teachers to develop skills, strategies and resources to work effectively in multi-ethnic, multilingual and multicultural classrooms.
3   Assistance for specialist staff in schools, funded under the Government's Section 11 provision. Their role is to ensure that the learning needs of black and other ethnic minority pupils are being effectively met through: home-school liaison; community links; teaching and teaching material which draw on a wide range of cultural backgrounds and

help black and ethnic minority pupils participate more fully in the classroom.

Weaknesses of the ILEA

The weaknesses of the ILEA are largely a mirror image of its strengths. The very size of the Authority which allows strategic planning and good central services has also created some rather cumbersome administrative structures and processes. These are both expensive in terms of administrative costs and create delay in decision making and delivery of the service. The very importance of the capital and its size attracts politicians wishing to establish themselves nationally. The innovative qualities of the Authority have attracted lively and radical teachers but at times have also allowed those radical teachers, and more important the unions representing them, to dominate the agenda.

In order to cope with the scale of the Authority's provision and differents needs and interest groups in an open manner the ILEA has created both structures and processes which sometimes make it inflexible, cumbersome and unable to react quickly. Consultative processes were created with the laudable objectives of involving those with a legitimate interest in improving the quality of decision making. Yet those very processes sometimes stifle and inhibit innovation. The ILEA spent one year consulting on the Hargreaves report, *Improving Secondary Schools*. At the end of that virtually no changes had been made to the recommendations. Meanwhile, other LEAs were already beginning to implement Hargreaves' ideas while the ILEA itself became caught up in the industrial action with the Inner London Teachers' Association, (the local branch of the NUT) which used 'Hargreaves' initiatives' as one area for non-cooperation.

Irritating as is consultation which leads to very long delays, it is a far lesser weakness than the consultation processes which lead to no action. Two areas which highlight this can be cited. First, in the area of tertiary development, local education pressure groups like the Islington Campaign for the Advancement of State Education were signalling as long ago as 1977 that tertiary colleges were needed. The Authority's response was to consider and discuss, to establish tertiary education boards, to provide sixth-form consortia arrangements, to defer to schools' desire to retain sixth forms, to consult not once but twice with elaborate machinery. At last in the Spring of 1987 the Authority submitted its first proposals for tertiary colleges in North East London to the Secretary of State, and in November 1987 the Secretary of State refused them all; for reasons presumably not entirely unconnected with its legislative proposals for inner London. In the meantime, young people have been ill-served in many cases by a variety of small and expensive sixth forms and diverse further education colleges to which, because of geographical location, they have had unequal access.

Schools' politics have been dominated since around the mid-1970s by the powerful Inner London Teachers' Association. Neither the national union nor the ILEA has really succeeded in controlling this London branch: each somewhat acrimoniously accusing the other of poor management or failing to act decisively. Such was the influence of the ILTA that the administration elected in 1981 conceded its power to move teachers between schools as school rolls changed. Instead they relied on 'voluntary' movement which resulted in the movement in 1986 of only five out of 800 teachers above authorised numbers. Only in the summer of 1987, faced with a budget crisis and an acute teacher shortage in some schools, did the Authority act to reassert its basic management right compulsorily to move staff to schools with shortages.

Profligacy in its administration and support services is a charge frequently levelled against the ILEA but one to which it has a number of good answers. First, administration in Chartered Institute of Public Finance and Accountability (CIPFA) and other statistics does not just include County Hall administrators but also professionals such as inspectors, educational welfare officers and educational psychologists who are providing direct support and advice to teachers and pupils. Second, costs are higher in inner London, both in the public and private sector. Therefore, the average architect or pay clerk costs more to employ than elsewhere. As I have already said the ILEA's provision for special needs is considerable, and this covers not just teachers and equipment but support staff like primary helpers and librarians who are counted as non-teaching staff, a category which is often wrongly equated with administrators. Further, because of its commitment to a comprehensive education service, the ILEA has an unequalled adult education service and considerable youth and community provision. All such provision inevitably needs administration: to employ and pay staff, to manage property and to control budgets. It is the volume of what the ILEA provides that is crucial in explaining its high expenditure.

Nevertheless, when this has been taken into account it is undoubtedly the case that the ILEA's expenditure including its administration is greater than the average elsewhere, or even that of other large inner city LEAs. The two chief reasons for that are; greater social need and higher costs in London. But the size of the authority and its style of operation also contribute. Because of its size the ILEA has ten local divisional offices whose main responsibilities are for certain administrative functions concerning schools. This means, however, that there are two tiers of administration with some duplication and the frequent need to seek approval of the central administration on relatively minor matters. That creates not only a financial cost but delay, which when attempting to recruit staff in shortage areas can be crucial. The other contributory factor is again the reverse side of one of the Authority's strengths: its openness and its commitment to consult and involve staff and consumers. There is probably no decision taken in the ILEA which does not involve consultation. As I have indicated ILEA consultation procedures involve expense and time. The end product could not necessarily be said to be a higher quality education service.

Standards

There is one further issue I should like to consider before going on to say something about the Government's ill-considered legislation on the ILEA. This is the question of the educational standards achieved in the ILEA. The Government has accused the ILEA of having low standards in spite of high spending. A careful examination of the evidence makes it quite clear that this accusation cannot be sustained. If no account is taken of the social and economic backgrounds of London children, then in crude league table terms, the performance of children in the ILEA is low. However, when the social circumstances of pupils are allowed for – and surely they should be – the ILEA is in the middle of the league table. According to John Gray and David Jesson at Sheffield University, using statistical techniques not dissimilar to those employed by the DES, the ILEA comes fifty-sixth out of ninety-six authorities. What is the Government doing about the forty LEAs below the ILEA? Are any of them to be abolished? It can in fact be claimed that in spite of deteriorating conditions in inner London with a substantial increase in the proportion of disadvantaged pupils in ILEA schools, standards have been maintained. As Peter Newsam recently pointed out 'A significant feature of exam results is how stable they have remained in changing and often unfavourable circumstances.' (*The Times Educational Supplement*, 29 January 1988).

After several years in which considerable emphasis was placed on initiatives to promote equal opportunities under the umbrella title of race, sex and class, the Authority then turned its attention in a more focused way to the quality of teaching in the classroom. It set out to identify weaknesses in its provision, such as inadequate homework policies in some secondary schools, and embarked on various initiatives involving the Inspectorate and others to improve matters. Work was clearly needed to restore the morale and confidence of both parents and teachers – especially in the secondary schools – after the long and damaging industrial action by teachers. Concern about secondary schools was reflected in Neil Fletcher's brave and honest comments soon after he became Leader. It seems somewhat paradoxical that he should then have had these remarks thrown back in his face by the Government and its friends when he had identified the very same problems as those identified by the Senior Chief Inspector in the DES, Eric Bolton, *and* was proposing that solutions should be found.

Turning to Eric Bolton's leaked report, it is interesting that his expert and professional view about standards in the ILEA differs somewhat from that of the Secretary of State for Education. He made the following comments. On schools he said:

> 'The ILEA's provision for under-fives is among the best in the country. After this, the mix of good, middle-of-the-road and bad is similar to that found in the country as a whole. While we judged two-thirds of what we saw to be satisfactory or good, there is some outstanding work in some schools and some that is very poor. Considerable time and energy are devoted to language, literacy and mathematics in all the schools seen . . . Overall the quality of ILEA's primary schools is similar to that found generally in the country.'

On secondary schools he was much more critical:

> 'Secondary education in the ILEA is generally rather poor though there are a few schools of high quality mainly in the voluntary sector. Of the 2500 lessons seen by HMI, 60 per cent were judged to be satisfactory or better, including 20 per cent that were good; 40 per cent were unsatisfactory or poor.'

Turning to non-advanced FE he stated:

> 'Standards of provision and work are generally good and in some cases excellent. Some of the FE in the ILEA is among the best in the country, for example catering at Westminster College. In our recent national survey on NAFE the proportion of good work seen in the ILEA's colleges was significantly higher than that for the country as a whole. The sector is buoyant and recruits students from all over London and beyond.'

About adult and continuing education he was even more complimentary:

> 'Overall ILEA's AE is a first-rate service in every respect. It is highly regarded by the many thousands of students who do benefit, or have benefited from it and regarded as an example by many observers of, and commentators on Adult and Continuing Education. Most of the work seen is judged excellent or good.'

Clearly there are weaknesses in the Authority's secondary provision. But the Senior Chief Inspector's report could hardly be taken as a warning about *overall* low standards.

Summarising what I have said so far, whilst there may be a case for working to achieve improvements in the ILEA – there is hardly a case for abolishing it. Moreover, abolition requires pragmatic consideration of whether the alternative arrangements would be better. If the answer might be that they would be worse, a responsible government would see whether there are other means, other than outright abolition, which would bring about the improvements it seeks. What other options might the Government have considered?

Options for Change

Had the Government left the ILEA intact as a unitary Authority, much of the change it wants would have been forced through by legislation other than that specifically aimed at the Authority. The changes, including rate-capping and compulsory competitive tendering, would have left the Authority (as many other LEAs) with much less influence over the system than it has now and with a tighter administration. It would still deal with capital building programmes. It would continue to be the employer of the staff in the schools and the colleges. It would still deal with admissions and have responsibilities for functions such as awards, the careers service and the education welfare service. Most important, it would still have its own Inspectorate. But a number of services would go. For example, it would lose its five polytechnics, its art colleges, and one large FE college; others would have to be curtailed because of enforced reduction of spending. Proposals for local financial management would give more autonomy to schools. A further consequence would be a slimmed down central administration making it more manageable and flexible. The imposition of a national curriculum would constrain ILEA politicians from interfering with the teaching processes and the content of what is taught in London schools and colleges. (I would like incidentally to stress that stories about such interference are based on malicious gossip and rumour and not on the facts.) But if they did interfere unduly, opting out would be possible. Taken together, the legislation would (whatever the negative effects on teaching in London schools) deal with most of the Conservative criticisms of the ILEA as it is now.

In spite of this, the Government has been determined to go ahead and unwilling to take into account the views of parents, headteachers or college principals. It is hard to see why it has been so hell-bent on abolition unless it is to destroy a public body which it sees as a challenge to its authority. The stark political facts of the matter are that an inner London-wide body elected on the existing system of 'first past the post' is likely to remain dominated by Labour for the foreseeable future.

There are five main reasons why a unitary authority rather than Borough LEAs would be better. First, the boroughs are too small to provide the range of high quality support services which are an essential part of provision, especially in deprived inner city areas. Second, the boroughs will find it difficult to attract the high calibre administrative and advisory staff which the ILEA has been able to recruit. Third, they will not be able to provide the range of educational provision, for example specialist music or adult education, nor will they be able to offer the same choice of schools to parents as the ILEA. Fourth, the record of some of the boroughs in relation to their management of existing services cannot give rise to much confidence about their performance as education authorities. Fifth, they have enough changes to contend with as a result of major new legislation affecting housing, employment practices and the financing of local government.

The Government attaches great importance to minimising costs and to maximising parental choice. Its plans for London will do neither. One consequence of a unified service for inner London is the extensive movement of pupils and students across borough boundaries. For example, at transfer from primary to secondary school, nearly 30 per cent of pupils move to a secondary school in a different borough from their primary school. This average masks some wide variations – in one borough, 62 per cent of pupils transfer out. In the case of FE students, only 28 per cent of students at ILEA colleges live in

the same borough as the college they attend. This long-standing
pattern of school and college attendance will create two
problems when forming thirteen LEAs from the ILEA. One is
the cost of the extra administrative arrangements which will
have to be established for recoupment between the new LEAs.
(There would be sixty-six possible pairs of bilateral
arrangements in inner London to replace the one ILEA
administrative structure.) The other is pupil choice. Parents are
free to apply for admission of their child to any school they
choose. In under-subscribed schools their child will be
admitted. In over-subscribed schools admissions are governed
by the LEA's admissions policy. Advocates of abolition often
cite this parental right in support of the argument that abolishing
ILEA will not affect the current right of parents to send their
children to any school in inner London. While this might be the
case for schools which are under-subscribed, it is less often
realised that this is unlikely to be so for over-subscribed schools.
Nearly all outer London boroughs give explicit priority in their
admissions arrangements to borough residents. New inner
London LEAs would not be any different. The result is that
parents who apply to a school which traditionally serves their
community, but which lies in a different borough, would find
that borough residents are given priority over their own
children, even if their children live closer to the school.

   The Government could have reformed the ILEA without
abolishing it. Other alternatives to giving the boroughs
education powers and thereby creating thirteen separate small
authorities could have been considered. The first would have
been to retain the ILEA as a single entity covering the same
geographical area as at present, but reforming it in a number of
ways. For example, there should be fewer elected members.
And there should be a substantial reduction in the size of the
administration, achieved partly by devolution of budgets to
schools and partly by the removal of certain responsibilities such
as the polytechnics. This option would have had the advantage
of continuity and would have avoided the disruption entailed in
abolition. More important it would have had the advantage of
retaining the many high quality services for which the Authority
has rightly been renowned, ranging from its provision for music

or special needs or adult education to its research and statistics branch.

The second would have been to create four education authorities in inner London. Each would cover a population of between about half a million and 650 000 people. As such they would have the advantage of being of a rather more manageable size than the existing Authority but would avoid the problem of being much too small as are the existing boroughs to run post-school education and specialist services on a cost effective basis. The main disadvantage of this option is that it would require a new political structure to run it. This might be a small joint board of representatives of the relevant boroughs or it might be small, directly elected authorities of seven to ten members. There would also be some loss of continuity and disruption, but the new authorities would be large enough to run an adequate system of post-school education.

The third option would have been to retain an authority across the existing geographical area covered by the ILEA to run those services where size is at a premium, but devolve those services, such as primary and secondary schools which can be run more easily by small boroughs. The powers of the boroughs would be limited so that they take no responsibility for colleges, the adult education service, special schools or the careers service. In each of these cases there are advantages in an inner London-wide service with levels of professional expertise that would not be possible to achieve by any borough on its own. In addition, primary and secondary schools in the borough education authorities might still be subject to inspection by the ILEA Inspectorate and their teachers have access to ILEA in-service training programmes. There are various possibilities for the constitution of such an authority. They include: direct election; a joint board; a joint committee, or a nominated board.

Of these three options the first of retaining the Authority is by far the best. However, either of the other two would have been better than what has been proposed. This constitutes a major reorganisation of local government in inner London in a tight timetable. Moreover, many would doubt the sanity of anyone proposing such a reorganisation in the very same year in which a radical reform of local government financing was being implemented. There is the prospect of large-scale disruption to inner London's education, complacent references to the apparent ease of GLC abolition notwithstanding. It is likely to be at least five years before the new administrative arrangements have settled down and the difficulties associated with reorganisation have been overcome. In these circumstances, the onus is on those proposing change to demonstrate that the new system is an improvement on the present arrangements, and markedly so, if the upheaval and expense involved in the change is to be justified. So far, this case has not been made. On the contrary there is serious risk of damage to the continuity and quality of education of pupils and students in London.

References

Gray J. and Jesson, D. (1987) 'Exam Results and Local Authority League Tables', *Education and Training UK*.

Hargreaves, D. (1984) *Improving Secondary Schools*. ILEA.

Inner London Education Authority (1985) *Improving Primary Schools*. ILEA.

Fish, J. (1985) *Educational Opportunities for All*. ILEA.

Newsam, P. (1988) article in *The Times Educational Supplement*, 29 January.

6

How Important is Choice in Education?

Denis Lawton

Introduction

We began our consideration of the 1988 Act with Stuart Maclure's analysis of some kinds of choice involved in 'opting in and opting out'. Other contributors have mentioned choice as an aspect of the 1988 shift in educational policy. To conclude this collection, I have responded to a suggestion from Basil Bernstein that some analysis of the idea of choice in the context of educational planning might be helpful.

In several parts of the world today it is being argued that choice is an important means of improving quality in education. Indeed, it is often taken for granted that greater choice in education is necessarily an advantage and will automatically improve quality. In this chapter I want to examine that idea together with some related questions about choice. First, I want to ask how important choice is as an aspect of educational provision; second, to look more closely at the *kinds* of choice that might have an influence on quality (bearing in mind that certain kinds of choice may restrict other choices or be harmful in some way); and third, given that some kinds of choice may be important, to examine whether the operation of the market in education is necessarily the best way of achieving choice and improving quality.

Background: The Cost of Education and Welfare

The debate about education, choice and market forces is part of a more general debate about the welfare state. Since the early 1970s, and especially since the oil crisis in 1973, there has been a tendency to look more critically at the ever increasing costs of the health service, housing and other features of the welfare society, including education. Many countries since the mid-1970s have tried to reduce public expenditure, and in England a critical review of spending on welfare services became official policy in 1979 with the election of the Conservative Government under Mrs Margaret Thatcher. Reductions in public expenditure have been achieved by cost-cutting, by campaigns to promote value for money, and by a variety of central devices to reduce local control over the allocation of resources (for example, rate-capping). Other solutions have also been discussed in the 1980s, sometimes with enthusiasm. One of them is to move further away from state monopolies or even state provision, by encouraging market forces to play a significant part. In areas like education and health where it appears to be the case that there are unlimited wants but limited resources, there is an obvious attraction in trying to cope with supply and demand by means of the market.

The Demand for Choice

Although the reduction of public expenditure has been a powerful factor behind some of these market discussions, there are other views which would support market choice in education. For example, during the Reagan administration in the USA, Chester Finn, Assistant Secretary in the Department of Education, argued that deliberately increasing parental choice would not only improve quality in education but would also be fairer to the majority, avoiding a situation where the only people to have choice are those who can afford to pay for it. His position was set out in a paper written by Patricia Lines and presented at an OECD Working Party on 'Quality in Education' in Paris in September 1986.

According to Lines there is growing popular support in the USA for educational choice. The advantages claimed include the following: greater parental involvement; enabling the system to cater for ethnic and religious minorities; and increasing opportunities for some poor and disadvantaged students. Her basic assumption was that families should be able to choose a school regardless of income. The common school tradition in the USA always conflicted to some extent with the American tradition of individualism, freedom of religion and choice in other spheres. In recent years migrant groups had become more vocal in their demands to retain aspects of their own culture and were increasingly resistant to the educational 'melting-pot' argument. Minority groups wanted to preserve their own religion or language, and thought that schools could have a role in this. Such competing demands put urban schools under great strain, making it questionable whether the common school could continue to cope.

Lines pointed out that private schools already existed in considerable numbers in the US; until the 1960s about 90 per cent of students in those schools were in Roman Catholic schools, but since that time the proportion has shifted: the number of students in Catholic schools has declined, whilst numbers in Protestant and secular private schools have increased.

Moreover, some parents already have choice by deciding to live in a particular area. In some parts of the USA other opportunities for choice already exist, including alternative schools, magnet schools, open enrolment systems, limited transfer options, inter-district transfers and 'home schools'. This kind of egalitarian argument in favour of choice of schools has not been very significant in England, but it could well become much more important in future.

In England, the usual justification for encouraging choice is that this would introduce the kind of competitiveness which would keep schools on their toes. The alleged need for schools to become more competitive is behind several of the provisions of the Education Reform Act 1988.

Kinds of Choice

Many of the discussions about choice are clouded by the existence of two kinds of choice, both of which are controversial. Arguments in favour of some kinds of choice should not be used in support of quite different kinds of choice in education.

Choice Within Schools

The first kind of choice is that available within a state school.

Although for many years the predominant pattern of school organisation was for children to proceed in lock-step covering the same curriculum at more or less the same speed, today it is generally accepted that children learn at different speeds, have different interests and tastes as well as abilities, and that these kinds of choice should be reflected in the structure of learning – to some extent. Ideas such as the national curriculum are based on the assumption that there are certain kinds of knowledge and experience that all should have. One of the best arguments in favour of a national curriculum is that is *restricts* choice: for example, HMI in England complained about the possibility of students dropping subjects like science or mathematics at age 14. (DES 1977).

How to cater for different children within a single organisation is highly controversial. In England, having eventually abandoned three different kinds of school (grammar, technical and modern) for three supposed kinds of ability, teachers have continued to dispute whether streaming, setting or mixed-ability groups are most effective. It is, however, accepted that any good school will be expected to cater for individual differences. All schools will offer some choices within and beyond the national curriculum, and it is generally agreed that this will be of considerable educational importance.

Choice Between Schools
How important is the second kind of choice – the opportunity for parents to choose a school? Parents may want choice for four reasons: first, because of the existence of bad or ineffective schools; second, because they want a school which will provide some kind of cultural transmission not available in main-stream schools – for example, instruction in a minority religion, or the language, literature and music of an ethinic minority group; third, because there is disagreement about what constitutes quality in education, parents may prefer one kind of quality to another (if both are available). There is a fourth important motive for choice: in the days of 11+ testing and allocation to grammar or other secondary school as a result, many parents disagreed with the selection and chose to buy a grammar school type of education in a private school. That situation has largely,

but not completely, disappeared, but it reinforced a tendency for parents to think of 'buying better' even if what they purchased was inferior, educationally, to state schooling. This kind of reason for choice has tended to degenerate into a less worthy attitude – snob appeal.

Each of these four categories of choice present educational planners with difficulties. If there are bad or ineffective schools, then presumably it is an educational administrator's duty to know about such inadequacies, put them right or close the school down. Bad schools should not be tolerated – for long.

The second category of choice (ethnic or religious teaching) is even more difficult. In the USA for example, the tradition until recently has been to expect state schools to perform a 'melting-pot' function: that is to Americanise the children of immigrants. Other countries, with or without immigrant children, have had similar objectives. For example, Norway and Sweden have a strong 'common schools, common culture' tradition. On the other hand, countries such as Holland have accepted and even encouraged, diversity of non-state schooling which is paid for or subsidised by the state. Other countries, like the UK, permit only some kinds of deviation from cultural norms, for example, Roman Catholic schools are subsidised but Islamic schools are not. At precisely the time when some Roman Catholics were arguing that it might be better for Roman Catholic children to be sent to secular state schools (leaving religious education to the Church and family) other minority groups were beginning to demand equality of treatment. The situation is by no means simple. Some would argue that just as female circumcision is not permitted within the National Health Service, so it should not become possible for the state to finance schools which inculcate values which are in opposition to the customs and laws of the host community. For example, would it be right to spend state money on a privately run school which deliberately fostered the idea of the inferior social position of girls? To 'deprive' an ethnic group of this privilege is presumably no different from denying Muslim men the right to have more than one legal wife? The argument is far from being settled, and the problem is not solved by forbidding such schools within the state system but permitting their existence as private institutions.

The third category, that is, a choice between schools representing different views of quality, is perhaps the least problematic. In rural areas such choices do not generally exist. If there is no choice of secondary school, parents either opt out, if they can afford to, or exert whatever pressure they can to alter the style or practices they dislike. It has been pointed out that better-off parents can in practice 'choose' a school by moving house. In recent years in the UK legislation (1980 and 1986 Acts) has encouraged choice between schools by requiring LEAs to provide parents with relevant information and opportunities for making a choice between the schools available. The probability is that most parents would accept a 'style' not entirely in keeping with their taste provided that general standards of efficiency were assured.

The fourth reason for wanting to have a choice of school – snob appeal – may be unworthy but is strongly felt by some parents. It is more important in the UK than in most other countries, and should not be under-estimated. For the majority of parents the real issue is whether the local school available is reasonably efficient and humane. Given those two conditions, most parents would not insist on choice. Exercising choice usually involves a 'price' in terms of travel and other inconvenience. It is probable that parents prefer to have good education available at the local school rather than have an opportunity to 'shop around'.

Education and Market Choice

Given that some, but not all, choice in education is desirable, we should now examine the possibility of using market forces to provide some kinds of choice. When politicians and others advocate extending market choice into education, they often fail to make clear what they have in mind. There are four basic positions on the market and education, each with possible sub-variants:

1   The most extreme 'free market' position would be to allow the market unrestrained influence by abolishing state provision altogether. Education would be completely privatised, and

schools would be run as charities, trusts, private companies or in some other way. Parents would have complete freedom of choice – within the constraints of their ability to pay. The state would have no involvement in maintaining standards or in financing schools directly or indirectly.

(*Choice 1*: completely free market – no state intervention.)

2   The second possible use of the market would be to have a completely privatised system of schooling, but include some kind of state supervision of the private system. The supervision could take a variety of forms: the state could legislate for minimum standards, including a national curriculum, and insist on all teachers being qualified; it could set up a national school inspectorate which would have the power to recommend the closure of unsatisfactory schools. Clearly the degree of government intervention could be light or extremely rigorous.

(*Choice 2:* free market constrained/regulated by the state.)

3   The third major possibility would be to have schools which are privately organised but are subsidised or paid for by the state (possibly be means of a voucher scheme). In the case of state financial involvement it would be very likely that the state would also be involved in regulation and/or inspection of schools. (HMI in England began in 1839 in precisely this way).

(*Choice 3:* private schools subsidised/paid for by state.)

4   The fourth possibility would be to have a system of education which was organised and paid for by the state, but which did not have any kind of monopoly and was subjected to competition. One version of this has long existed in the UK – that is, state schools are in competition with private schools. As we have already seen, this system leads to the criticism that choice is limited to those who can or will pay for it. Why not have choice for all parents by giving them some kind of access to the private system – and thus extend the market influence? This is the thinking behind some voucher systems. The 1980 and 1988 Education Acts have encouraged the increase in competition. The Assisted Places Scheme (1986) was a major innovation, and the 1988 Act introduces grant-maintained schools (GMS) which will have a semi-independent status; Mr

Baker has already invented city technology colleges (CTC) with more independence and a different kind of curriculum.

(*Choice 4:* Mixed economy – private schools and a variety of state schools.)

The arguments for and against introducing the above kinds of market choice into education are of two kinds: ideological and practical. I shall consider them separately, despite the obvious fact that 'practical' arguments about choice tend to be coloured by ideological views. The intention will be to determine what kinds of choice systems are appropriate to the UK in 1988 and after.

Ideological Views on Market Choice

George and Wilding (1974 and 1985) were interested in social values and the social and political ideas of writers on welfare: their study included references to education but was not directed specifically to questions of market choice in education. They classified writers on welfare into four groups (anti-collectivists, reluctant collectivists, Fabians and Marxists). In this way they related views on social welfare to social and political 'philosophies'. It is an excellent detailed study, extensively up-dated in 1985, and this summary cannot do justice to their comprehensive analysis. One interesting comment is their observation that between the publication of the first edition in 1974 and the revised version in 1985, anti-collectivism had emerged from obscurity to political prominence.

George and Wilding point out that all four groups give high priority to 'freedom' – but define it differently. Anti-collectivists see freedom in negative terms, as the absence of direct coercion – individuals can be starving but free . . . affluent but unfree. By contrast, reluctant collectivists use 'freedom' to mean freedom from want, squalor and other social evils. The Fabians regard inequality as a major threat to freedom; this implies a belief in government action to create and increase freedom (a view of freedom which is completely at odds with the anti-collectivist view). Tawney (1931) argued that the increase in freedom of ordinary men and women was due to an extension of government activity. The Marxist definition of freedom is broad but vague, focusing on the removal of obstacles to human emancipation and self-realisation.

The four ideological views of freedom imply different attitudes to equality: anti-collectivists are committed to inequality because they believe that attempts by governments to redistribute wealth must mean restrictions on freedom; inequality is also a necessary condition for economic growth. Reluctant collectivists believe in inequality but would like to see the levels reduced for social and humanitarian reasons – excessive inequalities exacerbate social divisions and offend human dignity. They approve of some government action to curb excessive inequality. Fabians and Marxists see equality as a central value of about equal weight to freedom.

Similarly, the four groups have quite different attitudes to the free market. Anti-collectivists see the market as the foundation of self-generating and spontaneous order in social affairs; it is also a vital bulwark of political freedom and the most efficient system of economic organisation. Governments should simply leave the market alone. Reluctant collectivists accept the effectiveness of capitalist mechanisms, especially the market, but are critical of *unregulated* capitalism. They do not accept the anti-collectivist view of the self-regulating market: without benevolent supervision the market may be wasteful and inefficient – it misallocates resources and fails to solve injustice and poverty, and without government action it will threaten political stability. Fabians regard private ownership of major enterprises and the inheritance of large amounts of capital as unethical. Most Fabians do not believe that a political system can operate without a money market, but advocate stronger regulation and controls than the reluctant collectivists. Marxists, however, condemn the free market system because it depends on oppression and exploitation and perpetuates privilege. They favour wholesale nationalisation, abolition of inherited wealth and confining the money market to the bare minimum. Free public provision would cover a wide range of goods and services.

In England there are continuing debates between the anti-collectivists and the reluctant collectivists within the Conservative Party, and between Fabians and Marxists within the Labour Party.

Nicholas Barr (1987) approaches the question from an economic point of view. There is an overlap with some of the George and Wilding analysis, but Barr is essentially concerned with the efficiency of market systems in delivering welfare services. Barr uses a different classificatory terminology but reaches similar conclusions to George and Wilding. Barr, in his approach to ideology and welfare, outlines three kinds of theory: Libertarian, Liberal, and Socialist. Barr also makes an important distinction between the amount of welfare and the means of delivering it. Unless you are either an extreme anti-collectivist (wanting to abolish the welfare state altogether), or a Marxist (wanting to abolish capitalism and market choice), the argument *should* be a purely practical (but highly technical) question of what is the most efficient method for 'delivering' the kind of welfare services (including education) which the majority of the population would regard as desirable. This leads us to the more practical questions about the market and education.

Practical Questions about the Market and Education

Having considered some of the ideological issues behind the debate on choice and the market in education, I would now like to consider the four main possibilities (as outlined above). What are the alleged benefits and the probable consequences (including the unintended consequences) of introducing such choices?

Choice 1 – Completely Free Market, No Government Intervention
This is difficult to envisage in 1988 because we have become accustomed to state provision. But in the early nineteenth century it was the dominant view. In England, 1833 was the turning point, (the first use of state money for schooling), and since then the story has been one of more and more public spending on education. It may be worth asking why the policy was changed in 1833 despite powerful opposition. Why was it abandoned? The free market in education was unquestionably failing to reach a high proportion of the population, was leaving young people less useful from a vocational point of view and

lacking in discipline – the pre-industrial techniques of
socialising the young to be obedient and to respect the property
of their betters simply did not function in the new tough urban
areas.

No advanced industrial society now operates with a system of
education depending completely on private organisations. This
is not to say that such a system would be impossible, but it is up
to those who advocate total privatisation to produce convincing
arguments. So far they have failed to do so. Most parents would
probably pay for schooling but inequality would be aggravated
(i.e. the rich would buy more and better; some would buy little
or nothing). There are other disadvantages such as economic
inefficiency – a modern industrial society needs educated
manpower. And apart from economic disadvantages, there are
good social and cultural reasons for state investment in
education.

> 'A pure market system is likely to be highly inefficient, and
> also inequitable to the extent that knowledge, power and
> access to capital markets are correlated with socio-
> economic status. Unrestricted market provision of
> education is theoretically implausible and, in practice, does
> not exist in any country.' (Barr 1987, pp. 311–12)

Choice 2 – Market Constrained by Government
If this option were chosen the state would not provide schools
but could control the private system by legislation (for example
compulsory attendance 5 to 16), a national curriculum and by
inspection. The government could also exercise control by
financial means such as subsidies or designated grants etc.

Once again it has to be stated that this arrangement has been
tried before in the UK, 1839 to 1870, and found wanting.
Matthew Arnold, one of the wisest of Her Majesty's Inspectors,
was completely convinced that the free market English system
was lagging seriously behind our industrial competitors,
particularly those he had studied, France and Prussia, where
superior planned systems were developing. Nevertheless it is
quite possible to envisage a privatised system of schooling,
operating within state guidelines, including a national

curriculum, and supervised by HMI. But it is difficult to see why such a system would be better than one provided by the state.

> 'Private production is likely to be efficient only if its quality is adequately policed. Libertarians dispute this view, arguing that dissatisfied parents could move their child to another school, and also that if a private school has a bad reputation it will go out of business. The weakness of this line of argument is two-fold. First, parents may not have sufficient information to realise that their child is being badly educated or, if they do, may not have the confidence to do anything about it. Second, education is not a repeatable experiment. It is true that a restaurant which provides bad service will go out of business; its former clients will have suffered nothing more than a bad meal, and can spend the rest of their lives going to better restaurants. But the application of this argument to education makes an unfounded leap in logic. Education is in large measure a once-and-for-all experience; a child who has had a year or two of bad education may never recover. In addition, a child may face a high emotional cost . . . in changing school. A more apt analogy is a restaurant which gives unknowing customers food so bad that it might cause permanent ill-health.' (Barr 1987, pp. 312–13)

A crucial factor is that private consumption decisions are efficient and equitable only if families have sufficient information and use it in the child's best interests. There is a high correlation between the likelihood of possessing information and socio-economic status. The most vocal demands for choice come mainly from more prosperous groups. Other problems include the greater wastage of talent among those who were poorly educated; and an increasingly dangerous social division between haves and have nots with consequent resentment.

Choice 3 – Private Schools Subsidised/Paid For by State (Vouchers)
In the USA and the UK, advocates of private schooling have

suggested that a more efficient way of providing state support would be to pay for or subsidise private schools rather than attempting to run schools by means of a centralised or decentralised bureaucratic machinery. For many years some critics of the state system have advocated various kinds of voucher schemes which would also encourage crossing the boundary between state and private education. In the USA Alum Rock was the only fully documented example of a voucher scheme in operation: it was not claimed as a great success and was abandoned after a trial period. In England, there was an extensive feasibility study in Kent, after which it was decided that a voucher system would be expensive and impracticable.

There are two kinds of voucher scheme – Friedman (1962) and Jencks (1970). The Friedman scheme would give a voucher to a parent covering the average cost of a place in a state school (or possibly a proportion of that cost). Parents would be free to spend the voucher at a state or private school and if necessary to 'top up' the voucher. Jencks advocated a more egalitarian voucher: topping up would not be allowed, but low income parents would receive a more valuable voucher, thus giving additional resources to those schools catering for children from poor backgrounds, i.e. positive discrimination.

Advocates of voucher schemes claim increased efficiency as well as parental satisfaction. In addition, parents using private schools would no longer have to pay twice. Barr disagrees:

'To opponents of voucher schemes their efficiency advantages are debatable and their equity effects almost certainly deleterious. The efficiency issue ... hinges on whether parents are sufficiently well informed to police the standards of their child's school and, if not, whether a publicly organised inspectorate will be more effective with public or private production. In equity terms it is argued that voucher schemes will increase inequalities in the distribution of education (both quantity and quality) by social class (though less so in the case of a Jencks type of scheme than under the Friedman proposals). Vouchers might well have advantages for middle class families, but only at the expense of less well informed choices by lower socio-economic groups.' (Barr, 1987, p. 353)

Choice 4 – Mixed Economy: Government Provision Plus Market Competition

This mixed provision has been the position in England and Wales since 1870. At present only about 6 or 7 per cent of pupils are in private schools. Since 1979 the policy has been to encourage the private system to expand, and to blur the distinction between state and private by the government subsidising or paying for 'bright' pupils from state schools transferring to certain approved private schools. (The Assisted Places Scheme – Education Act 1980). The operation of the Assisted Places Scheme in terms of giving additional choice has been criticised by Whitty *et al.* (1986). Promoting or using the Assisted Places Scheme inevitably indicates lack of confidence in the state system, especially comprehensive schools. It is the most obvious kind of return to a selective system of secondary education.

Should the state be even more expansive in what it would be willing to subsidise? (As in Holland where it is much easier for minority groups to set up schools and have them maintained by state grants.) The problem of general loss of social cohesion has to be weighed against minority group parental satisfaction; there are also unresolved ethical questions, already referred to earlier in this chapter.

In England and Wales, parental choice has been emphasised and extended by Education Acts passed in 1980, 1986 and 1988. According to the 1980 Education Act parents are entitled to express a choice for a school within the maintained sector, and to receive detailed information about the schools available. Preferences have to be met unless the school would be over-full or there is some other good reason. Parents have the right of appeal against a decision by the local education authority. The 1980 Act also established the Assisted Places Scheme, offering full or partial assistance with fees at approved private schools for children selected for their ability.

The 1988 Education Reform Act was only partly concerned with parental choice, although several provisions of the Act are in effect about introducing greater competitiveness into the school system, as Stuart Maclure pointed out in Chapter 1. For example, the national curriculum involves testing at 7, 11, 14 and 16, and schools will be required to publish results of assessment for the three older age groups. LEAs will be able to provide additional information about the catchment areas of schools (in order to alleviate the problem of crude league tables of schools being produced in the press, for example.) But the clear intention of the publication requirement was to provide information to parents as a basis for making comparisons between schools. The results produced by schools and LEAs, whilst not identifying individual pupils, will show what percentage of students performed at a specific level, subject by subject, and how that performance compares with other schools locally and nationally.

Most educationists are happy that parents should be provided with relevant information, although some, like Desmond Nuttall (Chapter 3), question the wisdom of unweighted test results being used as a basis for league tables of good and bad schools; and the possibility that parents will too hastily make decisions about abandoning low-achieving schools also worried Stuart Maclure in Chapter 1. Whilst some action may be necessary to improve some under-achieving schools, it will make local planning extremely difficult if choice operates against LEA planning objectives. The situation will be aggravated by other provisions of the 1988 Act, such as open enrolment and the ability for a school to 'opt out' of LEA planning arrangements by applying for grant-maintained status and direct funding from the DES. In order to avoid administrative chaos at the LEA level, the Secretary of State for Education will have to be very careful in approving applications for grant-maintained status, unless he really wants to undermine the present system. LEAs have a responsibility for planning the system as a whole and this is made difficult, if not impossible, if resources and numbers change dramatically in a way that could not be anticipated.

A real criticism of such measures, and of the other non-LEA type of school invented by Mr Baker – the city technology colleges – is that they are largely cosmetic. The picture may change for a minority of pupils, but the majority are left with no real choice. CTCs will almost inevitably result in selection, and therefore undermine the comprehensive system. In some respects it would be more logical to have a system based on Choice 3 (p. 112) – i.e. a market system which is tightly controlled by state regulation and inspection – rather than Choice 4 – a state system whose planning is undermined by unpredictable market choice. If Choice 3 became a political reality, then it would be desirable to press for something like a Jencks voucher scheme rather than allowing inequalities to increase.

Another criticism of some of the ERA 'choices' is that minority interests are fostered by such innovations as CTCs and grant-maintained schools, but that the quality of education for the majority is not being improved. Comprehensive schools were intended to promote social justice and societal cohesion; most examples of increasing choice in practice give more benefit to those who are already privileged, and by separating classes of children the aim of social cohesion is made more difficult. We are left with the problem of providing for 'desirable' real choices of the majority of pupils who will continue to attend the local state schools.

Choice for the Majority?

We should finally consider choice of two kinds within the state system: first, different kinds of school available for genuine differences (as opposed to desire for privilege); second, choices which ought to be made available within any good school.

A good system ought to provide, for example, boarding schools for children with real need of such provision – parents working abroad or single parents in difficult circumstances etc. (In fact the provision of state boarding places has declined in recent years in England.) The system should also cater for acknowledged needs such as interest and achievement in art or music. Some areas in the USA have established Magnet Schools in order to cater for individual differences, but they have found it difficult to avoid a status hierarchy developing out of the selection processes involved.

Other kinds of choice will be found within normal state schools. Good schools ought to be able to cater for a wide range of individual differencs within the structure of a national curriculum and beyond it. It is important to stress that a national curriculum is not a uniform curriculum. Good schools in many countries have begun to develop strategies for dealing with different kinds of ability, different styles of learning, different interests and tastes. In this respect the differences of the pupils are more important than the demands of the parents.

One major method is the modular curriculum in the UK (or the unit curriculum in Western Australia and elsewhere). Such developments may even be stimulated by the new national curriculum in England and Wales which, whilst specifying levels of achievement subject by subject, does not link achievement automatically to age. Thus more flexible timetabling arrangements will be called for rather than crude streaming and setting. A possible technique is the vertical grouping approach to timetabling which has been made possible by developments in computer programming (see Moon 1988). It is important to allow students to proceed at an appropriate pace without being generally labelled as 'clever' or 'slow'. Improved levels of assessment, including graded tests in appropriate (i.e. not all) subjects may also become increasingly important.

Conclusion

I began this chapter with some problems about choice in education. I questioned the assumption that all kinds of choice are desirable, and went on to analyse the effectiveness of the market in providing those kinds of choice regarded as desirable. Part of the problem is that because some kinds of choice are clearly beneficial, some writers have over-generalised by assuming that all choice in education is necessarily good. If that were the case, however, then some of the provisions of the 1988 Education Act would be mistaken, including the national curriculum. One major task is to distinguish carefully between desirable and undesirable choices. There is no reason to believe that the market is superior to planning in this respect. Those who advocate the free market as a good mechanism for achieving desirable choice, unfortunately often fail to clarify whether they mean a market which is completely free or constrained in various ways. If they do not mean a completely free market, then they have conceded a major point – namely that regulation and therefore planning may sometimes be superior to the market.

The Conservative Party is by no means united on the question of the amount of planning which is desirable in education, nor on the kind of planning. (For example, Keith Joseph advocated a national curriculum when he was Secretary of State for Education but later opposed Kenneth Baker's version of it as over-prescriptive.) Some Conservatives also seem to think that where educational planning is necessary, central planning is better than LEA planning. But one of the advantages of LEAs is that they encourage cooperation between schools rather than competition. Before sacrificing all the advantages of local planning, we should be convinced that the market, with or without some central direction, really can provide what is needed for all young people.

References

Arnold, M. (1869) *Culture and Anarchy*. Cambridge: Cambridge University Press.

Barr, N. (1987) *The Economics of the Welfare State*. London: Weidenfeld and Nicolson.

Department of Education and Science (1977) *Curriculum 11–16* (HMI Red Book One) London: HMSO.

Friedman, M. (1962) *Capitalism and Freedom*. Chicago: University of Chicago Press.

George, V. and Wilding, P. (1974) (revised 1985) *Ideology and Social Welfare*. London: Routledge and Kegan Paul.

Jencks (1970) *Education Vouchers: A Report on the Financing of Elementary Education by Grants to Parents*. Cambridge, Mass: Cambridge Centre for the Study of Public Policy.

Moon, R. (ed.) (1988) *Modular curriculum*. Paul Chapman.

Nuttall, D. L. and Armitage, P. (1985) *Moderating Instrument Research Project: A Summary*. BTEC.

Tawney, R. (1931) *Equality*. London: Allen and Unwin 1964.

Whitty, *et al.* (1986) 'Assisting Whom? Benefits and Costs of the Assisted Places Scheme'. *British Educational Research Journal* Conference Paper. Oxfordshire, Abingdon: Carfax Publishing Company.

Index